C000235891

"All of us could do with slowing dow
for our time in God's word in partic...... .... want to make progress
with Jesus, of course, but paradoxically it is by going slower with his
word that we will make the fastest progress with him. Linda's book is a
searching and timely call to meditate on God's word, explaining clearly
and carefully what that means and offering up a practical framework
to do it well. She is honest about the struggles of finding time for the
Scriptures but ambitious about the delight we can discover there. Don't
rush past this one."

ADRIAN REYNOLDS, *Pastor; Author; Associate National Director,*
Fellowship of Independent Evangelical Churches (FIEC)

"Linda has written a book that makes you want to put down her book and
pick up your Bible—there's not much higher praise to give than that. I
laughed (out loud and publicly), paused, prayed, highlighted and jotted
my way through this book. Linda warmly instils a sense of expectation
and joy at the privilege of mediating on Gods word."

GABRIELLE SAMUEL, *her. conference and London City Mission*

"This marvellous book must be given the time and space to draw us
into its thoroughly biblical, wholesome and potentially life-changing
approach. Reading *Deeper Still* has been a refreshing treat and has
provided an incentive to meditate more deeply on God's word, which I
pray will lead me to delight greatly in him."

RICHARD CUNNINGHAM, *Director, UCCF: the Christian Unions*

"This is just what we need: a call to replace our busy, anxious thoughts
with focused reflection on God's word. Linda Allcock helps us with this
practical guide to memorising, singing and speaking the word."

BILL JAMES, *Principal, London Seminary*

"*Deeper Still* is a highly readable and practical book on the richness of biblical meditation. In an age when we are surrounded by endless voices, this is a timely reminder of the importance of filling our hearts and minds with something real, deeper and ultimately far more satisfying."

STEVE McCLURE, *Ministry Leader, Navigators*

"Engagingly written and inspiringly simple, *Deeper Still* is a wonderfully clear and practical guide to engaging more fully with God through his word."

CLARE HEATH-WHYTE, *Author, Old Wives' Tales*

"Linda Allcock has provided us with a great tool for Bible meditation! With humility and clarity, she teaches us how we can fill our hearts with Scripture and ask questions to help the truth saturate our souls. You will not set down this book pessimistic about another spiritual task to accomplish, but you will be encouraged, instructed, and pointed to the grace of the gospel, which permeates Linda's chapters. I will be recommending this to many."

TAYLOR TURKINGTON, *Director of Women's Training Network, The Gospel Coalition*

"*Deeper Still* is a wonderfully encouraging, terrifically insightful and stunningly simple book. It is written to help us to find eternally satisfying nourishment through our daily encounter with the Lord in his word. As well as offering a simple framework to the reader to follow in achieving this goal, it is also honest, realistic and frank about the challenges there are. *Deeper Still* is also a brilliantly written and at times profoundly personal book. No matter where you are along your Christian journey, this book will be more than worth your time."

JONATHAN GEMMELL, *Director of Conferences and Resources, The Proclamation Trust*

Linda Allcock

DEEPER STILL

Deeper Still
© Linda Allcock, 2020

Published by:
The Good Book Company

thegoodbook.com | thegoodbook.co.uk
thegoodbook.com.au | thegoodbook.co.nz | thegoodbook.co.in

ISBN: 9781784984472 | Printed in the UK

Design by André Parker

Contents

Introduction

How quickly can you skim this introduction to work out whether you want to read this book?

You probably don't have long, so I'll cut to the chase. You're busy. We're all busy. Your schedule is full. And your mind is working on overdrive. You've got one hundred and one things you're trying to think, plan and remember—and another hundred and one things you'd really like to *stop* thinking about.

Most of us sense the same problem in our spiritual lives. I remember the day I discovered I could listen to a sermon podcast at 1.5x speed. New heights of efficiency! Listen to the same amount of teaching in less time? Awesome.

Or not.

Perhaps, like me, spending your days scanning e-mails and racing through life in general means that when you sit down to read your Bible, you struggle. You struggle to become immersed in the passage or respond emotionally; you find yourself having to re-read paragraphs and often can't remember what you've read a few hours later. When we skim, we may get a general sense of the meaning, but we miss out on really understanding, perceiving beauty and grasping complexity.

So when it comes to God's word, maybe it's less about 1.5x-ing it and more about slowing things down; giving ourselves completely to meditating deeply, slowly and carefully, so that God's word captivates our minds and moves our hearts.

That's biblical meditation. And that's what this book is about.

Biblical meditation will help you to go deeper into God's word, and help God's word to go deeper into you. It's a way to listen carefully, memorise, chew over and digest slowly what the Lord is saying to you.

Biblical meditation will still your mind. It's an opportunity to dial down the volume on your frantic thought-life and rest in God's unchanging truth. So that even when the Bible is not open in front of you, God's words are still at the fore-front of your mind.

Biblical meditation will fill your heart. It means listening to God's word in a way that impacts us deeply, so that we keep thinking about it throughout the day; soaking in God's truth so that it moves us to delight, empowers us to obey and enables us to hold fast.

And it's worth saying this: biblical meditation is not as hard as you may think. Meditation is not about spending hours and hours stuffing our heads full of Scripture but about coming to Jesus for life. As we look to him, we find not only the grace that forgives but the power to take God's words and live them out.

Before we get started, let me sketch the outline of where we're going. In section 1, *Still Your Mind*, we'll look at what biblical meditation is, and how it's different from secular versions. Section 2, *Fill Your Heart*, will equip you with a series of practical, simple steps that I hope will revive your daily Bible time as you "store up" God's word in your heart (Proverbs 2 v 1). Then in section 3, *Feed Day and Night*, we'll consider some passages that explicitly mention meditation and explore how they help us to live out the truth we hear in God's word throughout the day—particularly as we seek to delight in God, fight sin and endure suffering. I'd encourage you to read with a pen in hand to help you concentrate, question and remember.

Above all, my prayer is that this book will take you deeper still into the wonderful truths that God has revealed in his word, so that they fill your heart and fix your mind on him.

So please... don't just skim it.

SECTION 1

STILL YOUR MIND

CHAPTER 1

What is Meditation?

We're not really a museums sort of family. Our recent experience of the Imperial War Museum in London reminded me why. As I walked past a 1940s air-raid-shelter-come-dining-table with my husband and three boys, I was fascinated. "Can you *imagine* what it would have been like to have one of these in your home?" I thought to myself. "Imagine living with a constant reminder of the very real possibility of being bombed at any point…" I wanted to get inside the air raid shelter, to really feel what it would have been like to have all five of us crammed in there, straining to hear the bombers, terrified of what might happen next. I could feel my pulse beginning to race even as I looked at it.

Sadly, I had approximately 90 seconds to take in the exhibit—just enough time to skim-read the information panel. "Oh, an air raid shelter," was the extent of the engagement of certain members of the family, before they raced on to the next display, desperate to get the whole thing over with so that we could get to the best part of the day: McDonald's.

THE PROBLEM WITH SKIMMING

As frustrating as my visit to the Imperial War Museum was, it gives us a helpful impression of what biblical meditation is, and is not. Meditating on Scripture is more than just skimming the information panel to get the gist of what's going on before moving on. Meditation is thinking deeply about what it would have felt like.

The problem is that skimming is how we handle literature nowadays. I read recently that The New York Times on Sunday contains more information than the average 18th-century French nobleman would have learned in his lifetime![1] I'm not sure that can be verified, but the point is clear. We are increasingly overloaded with information—not just in the Sunday papers, but through the internet, emails, social media and advertising, even before we take into account all the other things we choose to read, watch or listen to. We cope with this bombardment by skimming—glancing through, trying to glean the important bits of information.

This all means that really reading and thinking deeply about what the Bible says does not come naturally. It takes deliberate effort to slow down and read each word—to get into the type of literature it is and feel the emotion, the suspense and the climax. This is why we need to relearn the art of meditation—slowing down and thinking deeply about what we are reading.

MENTAL DECLUTTER

It's not just our reading habits that have changed in the last few decades. Meditation has changed too…

In 1990 *The Oxford Dictionary* defined "meditate" as meaning: "1. To think about something deeply. 2. To reflect deeply on spiritual matters. 3. To plan, consider, or think of doing (something)."

Now that definition has changed. Notice what comes first in this definition from their online dictionary today:

1 Focus one's mind for a period of time, in silence or with the aid of chanting, for religious or spiritual purposes or as a method of relaxation.

1.1 (Meditate on/upon) Think deeply about (something).

1.2 (With object) Plan mentally; consider.[2]

Whereas previously meditation was to *think deeply about something* (the *something* being the important thing), it's now an exercise in *focusing the mind* (the mind itself being the important thing).

Why? Because of all the skimming!

Instead of thinking deeply on a few things, we are now overloading our minds with so much information that we need a new form of meditation to cope with it—a form that *empties* our minds.

It's easy to see parallels between our approach to information and our approach to material things. Previous generations used to consume much less, but really value what they consumed. My granny was a case in point. Everything was valuable. She used to wash out plastic bags and bits of foil so that they could be used and reused. The Christmas box was filled with old wrapping paper, often with three different Sellotape markings from years gone by. I once found a rag under the sink in the downstairs bathroom that in a previous life had been a pair of men's Y fronts!

That's thrifty (if slightly eccentric). My granny really valued each thing to the extent that she kept coming back to it again and again to get the most out of it.

Today we're more likely to "skim" stuff, just like we skim words: single-use plastics, throwaway packaging, clothing that we wear just a few times before chucking out and replacing with the latest trends. Our local authorities have to lay on advanced systems of waste disposal in order to keep up with the rubbish.

In a sense, that is what most people take meditation to mean nowadays: a way to empty our minds, dispose of the waste, and declutter all the information we've overloaded them with. And with the constant bombardment of emails, group chat messages, autosuggested YouTube videos, and targeted ads everywhere we turn… it's no surprise that meditation is increasingly attractive in our culture.

On hearing that I was writing a book on meditation, my neighbour John gave me an admiring didn't-know-you-were-into-yoga-chanting-retreats look, and commented: "Woah, interesting. It is very popular at the moment."

Another friend was excited because she relies heavily on the Headspace app, which helps people to practise mindfulness meditation. She imagined that I would be writing similar exercises to help Christians to de-stress.

When I said the word "meditation", each had assumed

that I meant emptying my mind (as in Oxford's online definition #1). For the sake of clarity, we will refer to this as "secular meditation" (although it's not strictly secular, as by this I mean all types of meditation that aren't biblical, even if they may be religious). This category includes the popular method of mindfulness meditation.

Distinct from that, we have what we'll call "biblical meditation". This is almost the opposite. Whereas secular meditation aims to *empty* the mind, with biblical meditation we are *filling* our minds with thoughts about a particular subject.

In the Bible's original language, the word means basically to talk with yourself; to think carefully about something; to take time to really engage with what it means. Essentially it is similar to definition #1 in the 1990 Oxford dictionary: "Thinking deeply about (something)".

As we dig more carefully into the Bible passages about meditation, we find that in all of the seven verses that are specific about it, it is the *heart* that meditates (a translation of the Hebrew word *leb*, meaning the centre not just of our emotions, but of our mind and will). The author John Piper explains biblical meditation like this: "'Meditation' in Hebrew means basically to speak or to mutter. When this is done in the heart it is called musing or meditation."[3]

In other words, biblical meditation is "talking with yourself in your heart".

This means that biblical meditation is more than just *studying*. It's more like getting inside the air raid shelter and feeling what it would have been like. Obviously, we can't literally get inside a Bible text. But we can ask those same questions that I was asking in the museum: "Can you imagine what it would have been like…?"

Can you imagine what it would have been like to have been Noah and his wife, hearing the first drops of rain after sitting inside an ark on dry land feeling like a muppet for seven long days?

Or to have stood near the cross as the sky went dark at midday for three long hours? 180 agonising minutes. 10,800 seconds. 1… 2… 3… 4… 5… Is this ever going to end?

Or to have been one of the women, unable to sleep, rising before dawn and walking to Jesus' tomb, desperately sad… only to find it empty?! The confusion, shock, sadness, grief?

So biblical meditation involves *feeling* God's word, but also *learning* God's words—or as Proverbs 7 v 3 puts it, "[writing] them on the tablet of your heart". This is far more than just *memorising* a text. After all, anyone can do that—and hate it! The seventeenth-century minister Richard Baxter makes the point that biblical meditation "stirs … the whole soul", not just the mind (*The Saints' Everlasting Rest*, p 188).

For the most part, I am like the child who races past the exhibits in the museum to get to McDonald's. I'm desperate to get my Bible reading out of the way so I can get on to the action of the day.

But there is no *better* part of the day! The psalmist describes God's word as "more precious to me than thousands of pieces of silver and gold" (Psalm 119 v 72). He's not racing past. He knows that meeting God in his word is truly precious. Why would I want to think about anything else?

EVERYBODY MEDITATES

Yet the reality is, I think about *a whole lot else*.

In this sense, you already know how to meditate. In fact, you already *do* meditate. You're already "talking with yourself in your heart". The problem is with what you're saying.

Just think for a moment about what you are thinking about…

"Did I lock the door? I don't remember locking the door. I always lock the door. It's probably locked. I should go and check. No, I'm sure it will be fine. But what if I didn't lock the door?!"

"They are so much better looking than me. This shirt really makes me look fat. I'm so slow at running. What's wrong with me?"

"The lead role in that box set—now they are hot. If only I looked like them." (Accompanying action = reaching for the low-cal smoothie for breakfast and the salad for lunch.) Or alternatively, "I'll never look as hot as them— what's the point of even trying? I can always start the diet tomorrow…" (Accompanying action = reaching for the large cheese feast pizza, half a tub of ice cream, the other half a tub of ice cream, and a sharing size bar of chocolate, all washed down with 2 litres of Coke.)

It's not just the anxious and jealous voices. There is also the proud soundtrack:

> *"He liked it. He said it was good. That moment*
> *when they clapped... I just want to relive that*
> *moment. I can do this!"*

Though there is a B-side to that one, called the I've-just-been-criticised soundtrack:

> *"I will never be able to write this book. No one will*
> *read past this chapter. I am so rubbish. Why did I*
> *even try?"*

And don't even get me started on the when-is-the-next-meal soundtrack!

> *"I'm hungry. Surely it's nearly lunchtime? That*
> *croissant looks so good. I don't need it. I already ate.*
> *I really need it. 10am, I'll wait till 10. How is it*
> *only 9:43?"*

Stopping to think about what we think about is especially important these days, because there are plenty of companies out there who are seeking to be one step ahead of us. I was unnerved by an advert for the entertainment provider NowTV on the side of a bus, which said: "We take your free time seriously". We used to have to choose which TV shows we watched, which newspaper we picked up, which books we read. But now such media is not sitting on a shelf waiting to be picked up—it is actively intruding into our headspace. And this is serious business. I open an internet page and I am bombarded not just with adverts, but targeted ads, using so-called "cookies". It's not a chocolatey treat that is out to tempt us, but a calculated invasion based on our search history. What that NowTV ad should really say is, "*We* are writing *our* words upon the tablet of your heart".

You can "talk with yourself in your heart" about the things of God; or you can "talk with yourself in your heart" about the things of NowTV. But you can't *not* meditate.

CHANGING OUR THINKING FROM ME TO HE

For the first 30 years of my life, the background chatter of my heart wasn't really noteworthy. But that changed when I developed post-natal depression after the birth of my third child. Life with three kids was busy, but life inside my mind was unbearable. The soundtrack in my head became a repeated refrain of: guilty, worthless, useless. As part of my treatment I was encouraged to really think about what I was thinking about. The chatter had become so dark and all-consuming, there was no way of pretending that my inner dialogue wasn't important.

If meditating is talking to ourselves in our hearts, then in the biblical sense of the word, everyone meditates. Our autopilot is to ponder our passions, desires and fears. The church leader Edmund Calamy recognised this back in the 17th century: "Like mill-stones [used to grind grain into flour] … the heart of man will always be grinding, always musing, always meditating".

The constant noise in our heads can be exhausting. For a lot of us, we don't like what we hear. This is why people in our culture are increasingly turning to secular meditation—they're desperate to declutter the voices from their heads. And who can blame them?

But as we'll see, there's actually a bigger problem with our thought soundtracks. They come in different tunes, but with the same essential content: it's all about me. Even when I'm thinking about *someone else*, it's almost always really about me.

Ironically, as I started to think about writing this book, I blogged my way through *my experience* of meditating on God's word: in the darkness of depression; in unexpected (and unwanted) life circumstances; in the battle to trust him in big life choices; in family life; in the fight against sin.

I started with me: "What does my experience teach me about this subject?" It was only as I was studying one of the meditations in the Bible, Psalm 104, that I noticed a simple but profound truth: the psalmist doesn't start each thought with *me me me*, but *he, he, he*.

I realised that I had started in the wrong place. I had to screw up my research, print off all of the Bible verses that mentioned meditation and start over. I had to change my thinking from *me* to *he*. What does *God* say that biblical meditation is?

My initial approach was like a parable of the problem. But biblical meditation doesn't delight in me. Biblical meditation writes God's word on our hearts so that we think about him; delight in him; want to spend all day, even all eternity, thinking about him.

To find a real solution to our soundtracks—to transform the thoughts of our hearts from *me* to *he*—would need a miracle. And God is in the business of working miracles.

CHAPTER 2

Silencing the Voices

I once made friends with a Danish student who was a huge fan of mindfulness meditation. She said it had cured her diseases and given her immense inner calm—and to be fair, she looked as if it had. She had bright, piercing eyes and exuded a quiet confidence as she enthused that I really should try mindfulness too.

Most of us would like to take a break from the stream of negative voices in our minds. My friend and millions of others claim that they're able to do that by practising mindfulness. In recent years there's been an explosion of books, apps, colouring books and even recipe kits claiming to help people become more mindful. So what exactly is this trend, and where has it come from?

The mindfulness boom began when Dr Jon Kabat-Zinn— an American researcher with a PhD in Molecular Biology, and a student of Zen Buddhism—realised he could bring meditation to a much broader audience by stripping it of its Buddhist elements. In the 1970s Kabat-Zinn developed Mindfulness Based Stress Reduction (MBSR), an eight-week course teaching secularised meditation. The model he built was simple, replicable and effective. Since then it has been woven into a number of medical therapies, and is widely used to treat conditions from depression, drug addiction and binge eating to asthma and psoriasis. Rather than explain what mindfulness is, let me give you a taste of it:

> If while washing dishes, we think only of the cup of tea that awaits us, thus hurrying to get the dishes out of the way as if they were a nuisance, then we are not "washing the dishes to wash the dishes." What's more, we are not alive during the time we are washing the dishes. In fact we are completely incapable of realizing the miracle of life while standing at the sink. If we can't wash the dishes, the chances are we won't be able to drink our tea either. While drinking the cup of tea, we will only be thinking of other things, barely aware of the cup in our hands. Thus we are sucked away into the future and we are incapable of actually living one minute of life. (Thich Nhat Hanh, *The Miracle of Mindfulness*, p 4)

Most of us have experienced this. We are carried away by the lie that if we can just get to that cup of tea, then we will be satisfied. But we all know that once we are there, our minds will be jumping ahead to the next thing. So mindfulness is about learning to be satisfied in the present.

The author Eckhart Tolle nails it with the title of his bestseller: *The Power of Now*. "Unease, anxiety, tension, stress, worry—all forms of fear—are caused by too much future

... Guilt, regret, resentment, grievances, sadness, bitterness, and all forms of nonforgiveness are caused by too much past" (*The Power of Now*, p 61). The solution, says Tolle, is mindfulness: living in the now.

Mindfulness meditation typically starts with breathing: noticing the rhythm, sounds and feeling of your own breath; listening for the background noises you normally zone out of; feeling the temperature of the room, the fabric against your skin; recognising the tension in your muscles and relaxing them one by one.

Another way to describe it is to picture the mind like a waterfall. The water is the torrent of thoughts and emotions running through our minds. It's as if we live with this constant flow crashing onto us. But mindfulness takes you into the space behind the waterfall, against the rockface—here you allow your thoughts to pass in front of you like a wall of water, without being impacted by them. And when you find yourself being carried away by the stream, you don't react, you just simply return to focusing on your breathing.

There is no doubt that this practice can be therapeutic. When I wake in the night, overwhelmed by feelings of "guilty, worthless, useless", I'll sometimes use some of those techniques to help me relax and drift back off to sleep—allowing those thoughts to pass by without engaging them, relaxing my muscles one by one, focusing on the feeling of the firm mattress beneath and the thick duvet above.

That said, there's a limit to who and how much it can help. Remember my Danish friend? As the conversation continued, it became clear that one painful struggle remained: her sister was battling serious depression. The sister had tried mindfulness meditation but couldn't manage it.

This encapsulates the essence of, and the problem with, any sort of secular meditation: it is something *I* do. Tolle promises that mindfulness will allow me to unlock "the radiant joy of Being" and give me a "deep, unshakeable peace". How? By accessing the "treasure within" (*The Power of Now*, p 12).

Secular meditation starts with me. Hence its popularity. It's something *I* can do to escape from the incessant voices in my head. If I can practise the techniques, and discipline my mind not to react to the negative thoughts passing through… if I can forget the pain of the past and disengage from future fears… then I can find peace.

But what if I can't? What if the struggle is too hard, the battle is too intense?

Biblical meditation is fundamentally different—and so much more hopeful. The treasure is from outside of us, not within us. We don't duck behind the waterfall and allow it to pass. Instead God steps in to transform the water's source.

DAM THOSE VOICES

After several days of eating off paper plates, reusing not-very-dirty items, and a lot of family arguments, my husband Jonty decided he would fix our broken dishwasher. He identified that the pump wasn't working (which is easy to write—the reality involved a small tsunami over the kitchen floor). He ordered a new pump and one more small flood later the dishwasher was fixed! We enjoyed four wonderful wash cycles, before the flood waters rose once again.

While he had fixed the immediate issue, the root of the problem remained.

Sometimes we try to do something similar when it comes to our thoughts and behaviour. "It is possible to change without God," writes the 17th-century Puritan writer John Owen. He calls this "an habitual change" and likens it to damming a stream (or temporarily fixing a dishwasher). By damming a stream you can change its course, but you will not change its nature. What is needed is internal renovation, so that the waters are "so cured by grace as that their properties, qualities, and inclinations, are all cleansed or renewed" (*The Grace and Duty of Being Spiritually Minded*, p 154).

Secular meditation offers a way to *modify* the content and pace of our incessant stream of thoughts. It helps us to *manage* the guilt, fear, stress, resentment, sadness and pain. But it does not, and cannot, fix the root of the problem.

THE SOURCE OF THE STREAM

If I'm honest, we never really got to the root of the dishwasher problem. We gave up and bought a new one. Mercifully, that is not Jesus' response to us. Instead, he correctly diagnoses the issue for us in Mark 7. He says that our thoughts come from our hearts; and that our hearts are faulty:

> *What comes out of a person is what defiles them. For it is from within, out of a person's heart, that evil thoughts come—sexual immorality, theft, murder, adultery, greed, malice, deceit, lewdness, envy, slander, arrogance and folly. All these evils come from inside and defile a person. (Mark 7 v 20-23)*

Jesus says that the waterfall of our thoughts is not a pure blue stream, gently flowing from its source high up in the mountains. Rather, it is a murky torrent of evil.

The problem is not actually the thoughts themselves but what they reveal about the source—that our hearts don't love God.

This all sounds a bit harsh, but when you stop and think about what you're thinking about, it is quite revealing. We've already noted that, essentially, I'm always thinking about me: my feelings, my rights, my desires. Even when I'm thinking about others, it's usually how they compare to me, how they have impacted me, what they might think of me.

But the problem goes deeper than the fact that my thoughts revolve around me. The real issue is that there is no thought of God. That's what "folly" means (v 22; see Psalm 14 v 1).

We haven't just forgotten him. The Bible describes the mind in its natural state as being "hostile to God; it *does not submit* to God's law, *nor can it* do so. Those who are in the realm of the flesh *cannot please God*" (Romans 8 v 7).

That's why secular meditation *cannot* lead us to God. There is nothing I can do to deal with the root of the problem— that my heart and mind love me, not God.

And while secular meditation offers to lead us to a space behind the waterfall of our evil thoughts, Jesus has a far more radical solution.

In fact, in Mark's Gospel we're given a glimpse of the cure even before we receive the diagnosis. In chapter 1 we're introduced to a leper. We don't even know his name. But we do know what his life would have been like. As someone with unclean skin, he was "defiled". The Old Testament law said he had to live outside of his community, in lonely places.

The uncleanness of his skin is intended to mirror the uncleanness of our hearts. And like us, the leper is powerless to clean himself up—he's powerless to deal with the root of the problem.

Then one day he hears of a man who can.

And so the leper comes to Jesus on his knees, begging: "If you are willing, you can make me clean" (Mark 1 v 40).

Jesus doesn't reach out and hand the leper a self-help guide to help him locate the space behind the waterfall. Nor does he encourage him to accept the hand that life has dealt him and start to live at peace with his circumstances.

No. Jesus reaches out to touch the man and says, "Be clean!" (v 41). "Immediately the leprosy left him and he was cleansed" (v 42).

The result? The man is cleansed, and is able to go about freely, "spreading the news" about Jesus (v 45).

And Jesus? He "could no longer enter a town openly but stayed outside in lonely places" (v 45).

In this we catch a glimpse of what the solution to our sin would cost. It took Jesus to the loneliest place in history, where he was abandoned by his Father to death. On the cross he took the full force of God's anger against the torrent of evil thoughts issuing from the hearts of humanity. And when it was done, he "breathed his last" (Mark 15 v 37). His heart stopped beating. His mind stopped thinking. The spring was extinguished. No more thoughts. Death.

Secular meditation leads us to a space behind the waterfall of our evil thoughts. Jesus leads us to the cross.

WHY I LOVE SELF-HELP

Which brings us back to the problem with secular meditation: it doesn't lead us to the cross. So while Christians are free to use those kinds of coping strategies, we mustn't stop there.

It's like my husband repairing the pump on my dishwasher. It offers a temporary fix. And if I was willing to manually empty the filthy water from the bottom of the dishwasher each time, and mop up the floor with some towels, then yes, we could keep going with the old machine. But to do that indefinitely is actually *keeping me* from facing up to the real problem. It's not leading me to take the cover off the motor and see that something far more serious is going on.

This is hard for me to say because I secretly *love* self-help books. My idea of fun is to go to the "psychology and self-help" section of our local library and look through a few titles. But I'm learning that by making life work more smoothly away from God, self-help may actually keep me from coming to him.

Tolle correctly identifies "guilt, fear, stress, resentment, sadness and pain" as problematic. But the Bible says that many of these feelings are actually an appropriate response to the problem of sin. The fact that all is not right, in the world or within us, is God's gracious prompt to lead us to repentance. But rather than dig deeper to recognise the root of the problem, Tolle's solution is to practise mindfulness, and allow the negative thoughts to pass.

Secular meditation will never shine the truth of God's word on my thoughts and expose what I'm thinking. It will never show me the consequences of living in rebellion against

God. It will never help me face up to the problem of death. Quite the opposite—it helps me to live in the now, so that I never have to think about the future. It seeks to minimise the impact of pain, hurt, sin and suffering.

Instead of waking me up to the fact that there is something deeply wrong with me for turning my back on God, secular meditation anaesthetises me so that I can keep on living my life away from God. Which means that, by itself, secular meditation will never lead me to the cross to see that there is forgiveness, and peace and power to change.

But there *is* a way of meditating that can…

LEAD ME TO THE CROSS

Earlier I leant you my headphones so that you could listen in to the soundtrack in my mind: "Useless, worthless, guilty, failure" is the mantra relentlessly reverberating around my head when I'm low.

For a long time I assumed that "useless, worthless, guilty, failure" was how God saw me too. I thought he must be so disappointed with me—I was such a terrible wife, mother, friend and Christian. Until one day, when I was in the bathroom humming one of those irritating kids' memory verse songs… and the words hit me like a ton of bricks. "God did not send his Son into the world to condemn the world, but to save the world through him" (John 3 v 17). I looked into the mirror and I realised that though I condemned myself, that was not God's verdict. The contrast between what God said and what I thought was stark. Was he wrong? Or was my thinking wrong? He sent his Son to save me—to take my sin in his body on the cross and give me his perfection. I believed that truth. And in that moment, it was as if the "useless, worthless, guilty, failure" thought disintegrated. Peace flooded my heart and mind.

I didn't realise it at the time, but I was meditating.

Meditation on God's truth exposed the lies that I was believing about myself—that I was useless and worthless because I didn't feel I was coping with motherhood—and led me to the cross. I saw that any and all my failures were taken by Jesus. He had given me his perfect life, and had sent his Spirit to empower me to love and care for little children as he did.

I could have managed my negative feelings through secular meditation. I could have allowed the thoughts of "guilty, worthless, useless" to pass by without engaging them. I could have stood in the bathroom and felt the cool tiles under my feet, smelled the bleach from where I had recently cleaned the toilet (if only), noticed the sounds of children beating each other up in the distance and, relaxing my muscles one by one, focused on my breathing: *IN for as long as it takes to say this sentence, OUT for as long as it takes to say this sentence.*

But that wouldn't have exposed the lies I was believing and it wouldn't have led me to the cross. It wouldn't have flooded my mind with the truth—and it is the truth that sets me free (John 8 v 32).

CHAPTER 3

The Mind that is
Life and Peace

We're almost ready to get to the nuts and bolts "how to" of biblical meditation. But don't panic, this is not going to be a DIY (Do It Yourself) manual. In fact, quite the opposite...

I used to look after a really cute three-year-old with a lisp, whose mantra was "my do it on mine own". To be honest, every three-year-old I have ever looked after has lived by that same mantra, and every adult I've encountered too. We just don't articulate it quite so cutely! We "do it on mine own" because whether we are three or 103, we don't want the sense of weakness associated with asking for help. We want the independence that comes from being able to govern our own lives.

We see this right at the start of the Bible in how the first humans react to the problem of shame. As a consequence of eating from the tree of the knowledge of good and evil, Adam and Eve's "eyes ... were opened, and they realised that they were naked" (Genesis 3 v 7). Their response? They made coverings for themselves. We love to *do*.

It was the same in Jesus' day. Soon after Jesus met the leper, he also met some Pharisees, who criticised him for hanging out with a crowd of outcasts and sinners. Jesus responded: "It is not the healthy who need a doctor, but those who are ill. I have not come to call the righteous, but sinners" (Mark 2 v 17). If those religious guys had a broken dishwasher, they'd have got down to "doing" straight away. They would be so busy mopping up the floor and emptying the filthy water from the bottom of the broken dishwasher, they wouldn't admit there was any problem. Jesus hasn't come for those who think they are ok. He has come for those who know they need him.

NO ONE EXCLUDED

One of the most precious parts of my struggle with depression has been that it has shown me how much I need Jesus. Seeing my weakness, feeling I can't do this, knowing I have nothing to give… In that place, the cross is the best news in the world.

The cross means that there is no one who is excluded, no leper too unclean. This is not too hard for anyone. Because as we come to Jesus, he doesn't say do, he says be: "Be clean". He has done it all—everything necessary to make us clean. By dying and rising for us, he has done everything necessary to bring our minds under a new governor—his Spirit.

Our minds used to be controlled by what the Bible calls the flesh (essentially the "me-monster"; the one that is constantly thinking about me). Romans 8 tells us that a Christian's flesh has been crucified with Christ, so that his Spirit takes up his rightful place as leader of our minds.

As Paul writes about this in Romans, he says: "The mind governed by the flesh is death, but the mind governed by the Spirit *is* life and peace" (8 v 6, my emphasis). In other words, life and peace are not something we reach for by our own effort. Paul says our minds *are* life and peace. (Isn't that an amazing truth? Just pause for a moment to stop and worship—you already have a mind of life and peace if you are trusting Christ. Wow!)

God does it all. He makes us new. Just as the whole universe orbits around him, our minds are now freed to join that orbit. This is the very thing that we were created for. When we move with his gravity, rather than pulling against it, we can breathe a sigh of relief. In that *is* life and peace.

Biblical meditation does not start with do. It starts with God—with what he has done for us. With who he has made us. In Christ we *are* clean; our minds *are* life and peace as he comes to live in us by his Spirit. Secular meditation doesn't just miss out on true life and peace. If it leads us away from the cross, it leads us *away* from the life and peace that can be ours in Christ.

The thing is, if we were to make biblical meditation all about "do" then it would be just as dangerous. The Pharisees were a case in point. They loved Scripture. They loved to learn it and recite it. They loved everything about it… except the very person it was about: Christ. They didn't want to come to him for life (John 5 v 39-40).

Properly understood, biblical meditation is about consciously knowing and experiencing the life and peace that are already ours through Christ. It's about allowing that life and peace to soak into every fibre of our being—our thoughts, heart, emotions and desires—so that it overflows into our decisions, actions and reactions as we walk in step with the Spirit. Every time we meditate on Scripture, we cannot help but be drawn to Christ, as we realise that we cannot perfectly live out God's perfect word. But Jesus did. In him we find the grace that forgives and the power to be transformed by the truth we are reading. We'll think more about this in section three.

REMEMBER WHO YOU ARE

"Ok," you might think, "But if this is true of me as a Christian, why is my mind still a stream of thoughts about anything and everything but Jesus? What's the solution to *that*?"

My husband has a weakness for Disney films, especially *The Lion King*. His favourite part is where Simba, the runaway heir to the throne, looks at his reflection in a pool and sees his late father staring back at him. His father rebukes him: "You have forgotten who you are and so have forgotten me… Remember who you are. You are my son, and the one true king. Remember who you are."

Remembering is how we orient our thinking and therefore our lives around God—remembering who he is, what he has done, and who we are in Christ. Instead of listening to the voices in our mind telling us all the things we are not, all the ways we have failed, comparing us to all the people better than us; instead of telling ourselves how great we are, recalling our achievements, chewing over the praises of others and reliving the applause; biblical meditation is turning from those voices to listen to the true voice—the voice of God. And only with him in the centre do we know who we were created to be.

Remembering and meditating often go hand-in-hand in the Bible. For example, in Psalm 143 when David's spirit is faint and his heart is dismayed, here's what he does: "I remember the days of long ago; I meditate on all your works and consider what your hands have done" (Psalm 143 v 5).

To show you how this "remembering" works, let me tell you about my most stressful day of last year—the day one member of the family "just topped up the coolant" before I left for an 80-mile drive to see friends in another city. 40 minutes later I was sat at the side of the road with the engine having overheated and exploded new coolant everywhere. Ironically, I had asked the staff team at our church to pray that this day would be as refreshing as a two-week holiday. I was so tired. I really needed a break.

But God did answer their prayer—in a sense. That morning, before I set off, I had reached Deuteronomy 4 in my Bible reading, having started in Genesis five months previously. Deuteronomy means "second law" (it's Moses' address to the Israelites before they enter the promised land—a detailed "Series 1 recap", if you like.) And not unlike the coolant, my mind exploded with how unbelievably awesome God's "law" is. Let me explain why…

REMEMBER WHO GOD IS

One of the things that had really puzzled me as I studied meditation in the Bible for this book was that almost half of the verses refer to meditating on "the law". Initially I took that to mean the Ten Commandments—which are a great way to live, but why would you meditate on a rule book?

What God showed me that morning through Deuteronomy 4 was that his law is not confined to the Ten Commandments. His law is the entire revelation of who he is from Genesis 1 through Exodus, Leviticus, Numbers and Deuteronomy. And as I thought back over everything I'd read in the previous months I was blown away by the awesome character of the God it revealed.

He is the Creator of the universe, down to every microscopic atom of our intricate bodies. He is the One who in wrath destroyed all but Noah and his family, because "every inclination of the thoughts of the human heart was only evil all the time" (Genesis 6 v 5). He is the God who raised Joseph up from the pit of the dungeon to the highest authority in Egypt (foreshadowing a greater leader who would be obedient to death and raised to highest authority). God is the One who looked with compassion on his people suffering in Egypt and showed his immense power even over Pharaoh through signs and wonders, culminating in the Passover—that terrifying combination of judgment, sacrifice and rescue. He rescued his people by bringing them through the Red Sea and bringing it down on the heads of his enemies. He broke out in wrath against the sinful grumbling of his people not once but four times in the desert. Through the thick, dark smoke he revealed his Ten Commandments—those ten simple yet comprehensive rules which underpin the basis of a flourishing and fair society.

38

All of this God gives to his people as his "law", saying: "Watch yourselves closely so that you do not forget the things your eyes have seen or let them fade from your heart as long as you live" (Deuteronomy 4 v 9).

This is the law—stories, true accounts of real history that reveal God's power, his character, his very heart. Moses summarises all of this saying, "Acknowledge and take to heart this day that the LORD is God in heaven above and on the earth below. There is no other" (Deuteronomy 4 v 39). We are to listen to, engage with, get inside these stories. We are to feel the suspense, gasp at the climax, recoil in horror at the shocks. *This* is what will captivate our hearts with the truth that the Lord is God in heaven and there is no other.

We are to meditate on these laws so that we will remember—not so much who we are, but who our God is. And we are to tell each other these stories, so that together we feel this truth and know that our Lord is God.

So even before we reach the first of the Ten Commandments in Deuteronomy 5—"You shall have no other gods before me" (v 7)—we've seen it already: there are no other gods before him. Indeed, this is why the Ten Commandments are prefaced by the words, "I am the LORD your God who brought you out of Egypt, out of the land of slavery" (v 6). *This is who I am,* says God, *and as you think deeply about that, all the other commandments will make total sense to you.*

As I read Deuteronomy 4 that morning, I can honestly say that God "[opened] my eyes that I might see wonderful things in [his] law" (Psalm 119 v 18). I didn't so much pray as just sit in stunned silence, thinking, "Woah. THIS is the law. This is God. And I can know him as I hear these stories of who he is."

Even as I freefell from that mountaintop two hours later, as I sat by the roadside waiting for the mechanic, I was looking at the words "DNF" I had written in biro on my hand to remind me: "Do Not Forget" all the Lord has done (Deuteronomy 4 v 9). Through the tears, I ran through in my mind what the Lord had done and asked him that even now he would be at work. And he was. Seven hours later I had successfully limped a very sick car home, stopping at every services to cool it down, with the heaters on full (in the middle of summer). But God was faithful. He kept me safe.

It was simultaneously the most stressful and refreshing day ever!

This is meditation: remembering. Knowing this great God. Not just knowing about him by learning a rule book but knowing him, by his Spirit, through the fullness of his law.

YOU'RE RESCUED—SO MEDITATE!

It takes a miracle to transform our thinking from me to he. But a miracle is what God has done. Biblical meditation is not something we do to save ourselves. It is something we do *because* we are saved. Just as the Israelites were given the law after they had been rescued from Egypt, so every specific example of meditation in the Bible underlines this fact. In each case it is one of God's rescued people who meditates— people who already belong to him, who have already received his promises. For example: Isaac, who "went out to the field one evening to meditate" (Genesis 24 v 63); Joshua and the people entering the promised land, who were told to "keep this Book of the Law always on your lips; meditate on it day and night, so that you may be careful to do everything written in it" (Joshua 1 v 8); David, who says, "I will meditate on your wonderful works" (Psalm 145 v 5); the musician Asaph, who sings, "I will consider all your works and meditate on all your mighty deeds" (Psalm 77 v 12); the psalm-writers known as the Sons of Korah, who resolve, "My mouth will speak wisdom; the meditation of my heart will give you understanding" (Psalm 49 v 3).

Only rescued people can meditate. And rescued people *should* meditate. John Owen speaks of how strange it is that the "generality of Christians are content to enter the promised land and then sit down just inside its borders". He sees it as utterly impossible that a Christian who has tasted the life and peace that are ours in Christ will not want to be "pressing forwards … to a full enjoyment of the precious things of the gospel, by growth … in faith and love, in the mortification of sin, in heavenly mindedness" (*The Grace and Duty of being Spiritually Minded*, p 193).

You have been rescued. You have been made clean. You have the Spirit within you. So don't sit down; don't sit back. Instead look back and remember who God is; then press forwards and enjoy the fullness of who he has made you to be.

SECTION 2

FILL YOUR HEART

SECTION 2

Introduction

My brother lived for many years in a remote part of Uzbekistan, in Central Asia. It was there he learned what Kilner jars are for. (You know the type—those big glass jars with a steel clip and a rubber-sealed, airtight lid.) I live in central London, where Kilner jars are mainly used for display purposes—in my case, I use them to make my granola look like it didn't come from a cheap supermarket!

But what Kilner jars are *really* for is storing up fruit and vegetables in the summer, so that when the winter comes and the market stalls are bare, you and your family can still eat… tomato pasta. Yes, my brother did indeed make 36 x 1.5 litre jars of preserved tomatoes all by himself, to feed his family through the winter. What a guy.

This principle of storing up is at the heart of meditation. We see this in Psalm 119 v 11 (ESV): "I have stored up your word in my heart, that I might not sin against you". But notice how meditation is more than *just* storing up. It is storing up God's word *so that* when we need it we can reach for it, find it right there on the shelf of our hearts and feed on it.

I love the way Donald Whitney highlights the importance of having the right truths from God's word stored up in our minds:

> The Word of God is the sword of the Spirit but the Holy Spirit cannot give you a weapon that you have not stored in the armoury of your mind. Imagine yourself in the midst of a decision and needing guidance, or struggling with a difficult temptation and needing victory. The Holy Spirit rushes to your mental arsenal, flings open the door, but all He finds is a John 3:16, a Genesis 1:1 and a Great Commission. Those are great swords but they are not for every battle. (*Spiritual Disciplines for the Christian Life*, p 40)

So in the remainder of this book, we will divide the process of meditation into:

- Fill your heart with the truth so you have it when you need it (this section).
- Feed on the truth day and night so you can live it out (section three).

To help us do this, in the chapters that follow we'll walk through Proverbs 2 v 1-6:

> *My son, if you accept my words*
> *and store up my commands within you,*
> *turning your ear to wisdom*
> *   and applying your heart to understanding—*
> *indeed, if you call out for insight*

> *and cry aloud for understanding,*
> *and if you look for it as for silver,*
>   *and search for it as for hidden treasure,*
> *then you will understand the fear of the LORD*
>   *and find the knowledge of God.*
> *For the LORD gives wisdom;*
>   *and from his mouth comes knowledge and*
> *understanding.*

This passage will form the basis of a five-step "meditation tool" to help us fill our hearts with truth, so we can feed on that truth day and night. I've summarised these steps as: Lord, Look, Turn, Learn, Live. We'll look at each one in turn in the chapters that follow. At the end of each chapter I'll give you a short summary of that step ("Meditation Tool"), as well as some worked examples to help you get the hang of it ("Putting It Into Practice"). The "P.S." sections offer you bonus tips and ideas.

As I was writing this book I was encouraged to neaten things up by making each step a verb (so it would become, "Ask, Look, Turn, Learn, Live"). But I couldn't get away from the fact that we must start with the Lord. Jesus doesn't say "do", he says "be". This is not a "technique" to master. Meditation is all about Christ—what he has done and what he continues to do as he reveals his wisdom to us.

If you've never read the Bible much before, then I hope these steps are simple enough to get you started. Think of it a bit like one of those "couch to 5k" learn-to-run training programmes. And if you are already "running"—regularly reading the Bible—then you may want to set aside extra time to go deeper into what the Bible says, and let it go deeper into you, either as a regular or occasional exercise. This tool would be great to use as you prepare to hear the sermon on Sunday, for example.

Finally, remember that this tool is only intended as scaffolding. It is designed to help you build the house, rather than as an end in itself. The aim is that after a little while you won't need the scaffolding, as Bible reading and meditation become more natural to you. Don't worry if you run out of time to get through all of these categories, or you can't think of an example for one of them, and don't let this scaffold constrain you. The precise "how" is not important—what matters is that you store God's word in your heart, so that you can take it with you into your day.

CHAPTER 4

The Lord Gives Wisdom

Lord | Look | Turn | Learn | Live

If you call out for insight
and cry aloud for understanding…
Proverbs 2 v 3

We've already established that in our house, we love a good Disney-style movie: the songs, the feel-good factor, the inevitable happy ending. So I was pretty excited to watch *Joseph King of Dreams*—a DreamWorks retelling of Genesis 37 – 50.

I had mentally prepared myself for the slushy sentimentalism and shocking corruption of the storyline that you inevitably get with any mainstream interpretation of a Bible story.

What I was not prepared for, however, was the theological punch of the film's signature song. It's a beautiful, haunting hymn of faith sung by Joseph from his dark prison cell, with a repeated refrain of, "You know better than I". The song marks a turning point for Joseph, where he lets go of his self-sufficiency, and admits that he doesn't know the answers and that he needs God's help.

I was stunned into silence, in awe of the way that God could embed such a foundational truth in mainstream media, in a culture constantly humming, "I know better than you".

Back in the days of Proverbs they were singing the same song. Solomon, the writer of Proverbs, describes the people's response to God's offer of wisdom in 1 v 24: "You refuse to listen when I call and no one pays attention when I stretch out my hand". It's as if God is calling out, offering wisdom, and people are walking on by, paying no attention, humming "I know better than you".

So, in Proverbs 2 v 1-6 Solomon knows that he has to teach his sons how to listen. He urges them repeatedly: *The Lord gives wisdom, so ask him for it!* This is something Solomon has experienced first-hand. As the king of Israel, Solomon was famed for his wisdom—kings and queens came from the ends of the earth to listen to him. Yet when the queen of Sheba—ruler of one of the greatest empires of that time— listened, she responded: "Praise be to the LORD your God" (1 Kings 10 v 9). Solomon's wisdom came from God. He was wise because he had called out for insight and cried aloud for understanding.

And so must we—because, like the sons in Proverbs 2, we have an attitude problem. As we come to open God's word, we must recognise that we are rebellious by nature. We think we know better. Our ears do not naturally turn towards God. Our hearts incline towards other lovers, we are lazy in our listening, and even when we *do* listen, we often forget what we have learned.

A large part of the reason why we are not changed by our time with God; why we don't remember what we've read; why we don't long to meet with God is that we don't start with the Lord. We start with ourselves. We think we know. So we don't ask him for insight. We rely on our own understanding.

LOWER YOUR EXPECTATIONS (OF YOURSELF)

Rather than telling them to depend on their own abilities, Solomon implores his sons to "call out for insight and cry aloud for understanding!" (v 3). *You need help, so cry out for it!*

There is one member of our family who excels at this: my baby niece, Anastasia. When she came to stay, she was an expert at crying out from her crib. She knew that she needed help. She couldn't get out by herself, she couldn't feed herself, she couldn't change herself—she needed me. And she was not afraid to cry… *loudly!*

What Solomon has in mind is no token "pray before you start reading the Bible" but a loud, heartfelt SHOUT for help like Anastasia's. So the common description of personal Bible reading as a "quiet time" couldn't be more wrong!

When did you last "call out" for insight as you opened the Bible? Calling out is what we do when there is a need—a fire or an emergency of some kind. Have you ever felt the emergency of needing to know God but not having the resources yourself to understand his word?

When did you last "cry aloud" for understanding? In our culture we tend to prefer to pray silently, but why not give praying out loud a go? Ask. Loudly! It will feel very weird, I can assure you! But should it? If we knew how badly we needed help, maybe we would shout aloud to the Lord with a greater urgency.

In the Gospels Jesus picks up the image of a little child. Right before he calls people to come to him with his famous invitation, "Come to me, all you who are weary and burdened, and I will give you rest," he prays, "I praise you, Father, Lord of heaven and earth, because you have hidden these things from the wise and learned, and revealed them to little children" (Matthew 11 v 28, 25).

God reveals himself to those who will come like little children: knowing their need, asking for help. And—perhaps more shocking still—God hides that knowledge from the wise and learned who think they've got it covered.

We must beware of the attitude of the world that hums "I know better than you". God reveals himself to those who are like little children: to those who know their need, who will call out to him for insight and cry aloud for understanding.

Often I am not moved by what I read in God's word because I have arrogantly opened up the page armed with my own expertise. My unspoken assumption is, "I know better than you". And so my heart is not stirred by what I read—it's just words on a page, or an English comprehension activity to be completed.

On the other hand, it may be that you are new to Bible reading and you genuinely know that you cannot understand it by yourself. Perhaps you are reading this book in the hope that you can become "wise and learned", or pick up a technique to help you understand. But we can never hope to understand God's word on our own. So be encouraged. The Lord gives wisdom; he speaks by his Spirit. All we have to do is ask.

We need to pause before we open our Bibles to *lower* our expectations—of ourselves. We are merely little children: ignorant, helpless, needy. We must recognise that however many times we've read a passage before, and whether we are Bible scholars or baby Christians, we cannot know God unless he gives us wisdom and understanding. So we must call out for insight.

RAISE YOUR EXPECTATIONS (OF GOD)

Solomon's instruction to his son comes with a wonderful promise: "If you call out for insight and cry aloud for understanding ... *then* you will understand the fear of the LORD and find the knowledge of God. For the LORD gives wisdom; from his mouth come knowledge and understanding" (Proverbs 2 v 3, 5-6, my italics). We need to pause before we open our Bibles to *raise* our expectations: through this book the Spirit speaks; through this book we can know God!

These phrases "fear of the LORD" and "knowledge of God" are Torah words (from the first five books of the Old Testament). They speak not of a cerebral knowledge of God, but a heartfelt experience. You can see this in Deuteronomy 4 v 34-35. We can almost sense Moses' heart overflowing as he explains:

> *Has any god ever tried to take for himself one*
> *nation out of another nation, by testings, by signs*
> *and wonders, by war, by a mighty hand and an*
> *outstretched arm, or by great and awesome deeds,*
> *like all the things the LORD your God did for you in*
> *Egypt before your very eyes? You were shown these*

things so that you might know that the LORD is God;
besides him there is no other.

There is an old saying: tell me and I forget, show me and I remember, involve me and I understand. By the time the people get to Deuteronomy 5 and hear the Ten Commandments, they hardly need to be *told* "You shall have no other gods before me" because they have been *shown* that there is no other god like him. They have been *involved*—their own eyes have seen through his signs and wonders, through battles won by his mighty arm acting on their behalf. Their hearts have trembled with fear already at his great and awesome deeds.

This is what it means for God to give us insight. This is what we are calling out for. Not just that God would *tell* us about himself through his word, but that he would *show* us through the stories, poetry and songs in Scripture who he really is. That he would *involve* us in the unfolding story of his great and awesome deeds to rescue a people from slavery to sin and death through the sacrifice of his own Son.

As I open up God's word, I aim far too low. I am content just to know facts about him. I need to raise my expectations. Far more than a comprehension exercise to be conquered, opening our Bible and crying "Lord" means that we can and will find something wonderful: "the knowledge of God".

KNOW HIM AS FATHER

The New Testament explains in more detail what is hinted at in the father-son language in Proverbs. In the Sermon on the Mount (Matthew 5 – 7), Jesus goes up a mountain and expounds the law to his people assembled around (a scene that echoes Moses giving the law at Mount Sinai). In what we now call "The Lord's Prayer", Jesus teaches his disciples to approach the Lord as "Our Father in heaven". It's a beautiful phrase that captures perfectly the aim of knowing God and fearing him rightly.

Through Christ, we can know God in a fuller way—not just as Lord, but as our Father. Just think of the intimacy and privilege of that word. In some respects, the idea that we can know God is a shocking suggestion. By nature we're among those who "refuse to listen" (Proverbs 1 v 24)—there is no way that we deserve to know God.

Yet when we turn to Christ—when the Spirit enables us to admit our own inadequacy and cry out to Jesus for rescue— we become God's children. The relationship we could never earn is given to us as Jesus takes our rebellion on himself on the cross so that we can be forgiven and brought into the relationship he has with his Father. Which means that as we come to God day by day, we are no longer calling out "Lord" from a distance but from the position of a much-loved child, with whom God delights to share himself.

FEAR HIM AS OUR FATHER IN HEAVEN

I love the way that Jesus gently reminds us not to take this access for granted though. God is our Father, but he is "our Father *in heaven*" (Matthew 6 v 9).

I have a wonderful Jewish friend, and once in conversation as I spoke about God I called him "Yahweh" (the name for God which is translated in our English Bibles as LORD).

She was visibly shocked. She explained that she was brought up to regard God's name with so much reverence, awe and respect that they wouldn't use it in conversation.

I was really struck by her understanding of God. In some ways she was right—God is in heaven, so he is to be massively respected and revered, and I should be in awe of him. I can get so overfamiliar with calling God "Father" that I forget how powerful he is. His name is awesome. Although the words "awful" and "awesome" have come to mean opposite things, originally, their meanings were more similar. God is closer to "awful" than we often imagine him as—in the sense that he is terrifying and fearsome. We are prone to forget that.

Ecclesiastes 5 puts it like this:

> *Guard your steps when you go to the house of God.*
> *Go near to listen rather than to offer the sacrifice of*
> *fools, who do not know that they do wrong. Do not*
> *be quick with your mouth, do not be hasty in your*
> *heart to utter anything before God. God is in heaven*
> *and you are on earth, so let your words be few.*
> *(Ecclesiastes 5 v 1-2)*

We are to guard our hearts and our mouths—to carefully consider who it is that we approach. "The fear of the LORD is the beginning of wisdom" (Proverbs 9 v 1). If an earthly father should have the respect of his children, how much more should our Father in heaven have our respect! And it is this reverence that moves our hearts to hear and do what he commands.

FERVENT CRIES

Stop for a moment and think about your heart attitude towards God's word. When did you last open his word? How did you feel about it? As you come to the Bible, are your first words "Lord, help me"? Or are they "I've got this covered"?

We need to lower ourselves, and confess our arrogance and sin. It is so wrong when we approach God humming "I know better than you"; when we don't cry out for help; when we come to his word armed with our own knowledge, rather than feeling our need of God. Hebrews tells us that even Jesus, in his "life on earth … offered up prayers and petitions with fervent cries and tears to the one who could save him from death, and he was heard because of his reverent submission" (Hebrews 5 v 7). If Jesus needed to reverently submit to his Father and cry fervently for help, why do I feel that I don't need to? How wrong I am.

And we need to raise our expectations, coming to God's word excited to be shown and involved anew in the unfolding story—not of what I am doing in this world, but of what the Lord is doing in this world. We are to long to be a part of that as we enjoy him as our Father and fear him as our Father in heaven.

I find this so hard that I'm thinking of writing over the front of my Bible in Sharpie: "Call out for insight!"

In the meantime, I've decided to set my phone alarm to go off every hour as I write this, just to remind me to call out for insight. I need to break my old habits of arrogance and competence. I need wisdom—and the Lord generously gives it.

MEDITATION TOOL: LORD

- Start with the Lord—not yourself. The Lord alone gives wisdom—so call out for insight.
- Lower your expectations of yourself and raise your expectations of God.

PUTTING IT INTO PRACTICE

- Quieten your mind and consider who you approach. Lower your expectations of yourself (maybe even kneel). You cannot understand without the Lord's help.
- Start this time by crying out *Lord!* Call out for the insight that you need; confess where you have thought that you know better.
- Raise your expectations—through meditating on his word you can know and fear our Father in heaven.

P.S. BODY POSTURE MATTERS

Studying methods of meditation from Christians throughout history, it is striking how much emphasis they place on careful preparation. For example, the method developed by 16th-century priest Ignatius of Loyola recommends: "Before the place of meditation make an act of reverence or humility. Start the meditation on my knees, now prostrate on the earth …"[4]

I suspect this emphasis on preparation stems from not understanding that Christ alone prepares us to meet with God. But does our confidence in Christ veer into an over-familiarity? I imagine that few of us reading this would consider lying flat on the ground to pray, yet that was precisely the position of Peter when he realised Jesus' power (Luke 5 v 8), and of the women who first met the risen Jesus (Matthew 28 v 9). Yes, immediately Jesus told them, "Do not be afraid". But have you ever considered God to be so fearsome that even lying prostrate is not a humble enough stance to express his worth and our wretchedness? Physically kneeling down as we "call out for insight" can be a powerful physical representation of our need.

Body posture matters. Body, heart and mind are connected. It's hard to listen attentively while lying in bed, or on a crowded bus. It says a lot about my heart attitude to a person if I only ever speak to them when doing something else!

CHAPTER 5

Look for Truth as for Treasure

Lord | **Look** | Turn | Learn | Live

Look for it as for silver
and search for it as for hidden treasure…
Proverbs 2 v 4

As a child, I used to love treasure hunting. My great hope was to one day buy a metal detector. I remember going to the beach in France one year and searching and searching until eventually I found a 10 Franc coin, which I used to purchase a bar of Milka chocolate.

The next year I had the childish expectation that having found treasure once, I would find it again. Through much determination, time, and traipsing up and down, sifting my way through broken bottles, dead crabs, shells and who knows what else, I found another 10F coin! Unbelievable!

Was it unbelievable? Or was it that my joy at the previous find had spurred me on to persevere in looking, to expend whatever time it took until I was successful? I do love Milka, so was pretty determined to stop at nothing until I found the necessary coin to secure another bar. (Though I have a sneaking suspicion that my dad might have planted the coin for fear that we would end up missing the ferry!)

As we open God's word, do we believe there is treasure there? If we did, we might treat our Bible times differently. We would look forward to reading the Bible with anticipation and excitement. We would, as Proverbs 2 v 4 says, "Look for [insight and understanding] as for silver and search for it as for hidden treasure". We would dig into the passage with commitment and perseverance. And when we found the promised treasure, we would respond in joyful prayer and thankfulness.

John Owen makes the point that seeing meditation as searching for treasure creates in us an appetite for more:

> When the soul hath at any time tasted that the Lord is gracious, when its meditations on him have been sweet … hereon [the soul] comes unto this duty [of reading Scripture] with *earnest desires* to have the like tastes. (*The Grace and Duty of Being Spiritually Minded*, p 132)

Too often I come to God's word expectant, yes—but only to be able to tick the box on my reading plan. Committed, yes—but only to getting this out of the way so I can get on to the real work of the day. Determined, yes—but only to work through my daily routine of reading a chapter, writing a few sentences about it and praying. There is no excitement or anticipation, no real desire to meet with God and taste and see his goodness. I have settled into a rut. And I rarely find treasure in the rut.

TOOLS HELP US SEARCH

So if we feel like we're in a rut, how do we get out of it? How do we find the treasure in God's word?

If you are going to search, you need tools (hence why I was saving up for a metal detector!). There are lots of "tools" available to help you read the Bible—different steps, frameworks or study guides to help you to think about a passage and understand what it means. Feel free to use whatever you have found helpful. One that I use, which is particularly geared towards meditation, is to look at the passage through three lenses: *God, Christ, Us*. You simply read the passage asking: What do we learn about *God*? How do we glimpse *Christ*? What did it mean for the *first hearers* and therefore for *us*? Let's walk through each of those lenses in turn.

WHAT DOES THIS TEACH ME ABOUT <u>GOD</u>?

The Bible is a book first and foremost about God. That might sound obvious, but so often we read it as if it were primarily about us. For example, my first Bible had a section at the front called "Where to find help when…" where it listed a whole load of life circumstances and relevant Bible passages. It was a nice sentiment, and helpful in some senses, but that shouldn't be how we normally approach the Bible. Scripture is not a self-help book written to help me sort my life out. Rather, it is a book about how great God is. Looking for what a text teaches about God reminds us each time we come to the Bible that this is first and foremost about *him*.

This means asking questions like: What do these verses teach me about God's character? What do they tell me about his priorities and his plans? What are the things he loves and the things that grieve him?

HOW DO WE GLIMPSE <u>CHRIST</u>?

My friend has a beautiful line drawing of a garden on the wall of her conservatory. I once commented how beautiful it was, to which she replied, "Look out of the window". It turns out that it was the architect's line drawing of the plan for her garden. As beautiful as the plan was, the garden brought the picture to life.

In many ways, the Old Testament is like that line drawing—it's a beautiful sketch of God, his character, his works and his promise. But all those things are brought to life in a new way when we look "through the window" at the person of Christ. His life, death, resurrection and ascension are what the entirety of Scripture is pointing to. He said as much to his disciples: "'Did not the Messiah have to suffer these things and then enter his glory?' And beginning with Moses and all the Prophets, he explained to them what was said in all the Scriptures concerning himself" (Luke 24 v 26-27). Or in other words: *The line drawing is of me.*

So, good questions to ask as we read the Old Testament include: How does this point me to Christ? How does it move me to worship him?

Matthew gives us some helpful pointers in the opening verse of the New Testament, where he introduces "Jesus the Messiah, the Son of David, the Son of Abraham" (Matthew 1 v 1). Everything that comes before that point—the whole Old Testament—will give us glimpses of the chosen One

God promised to send (Messiah); the greater King (Son of King David); and the One who would be the answer to all of God's promises (made to Abraham). So for example, as we read 1 Samuel 17, where King David wins the victory for his people over the enemy Goliath, we glimpse the greater King, the Son of David, who rescues us from our enemies—sin, death and the devil.

Even if we struggle to spot these themes in an Old Testament passage, most Bibles have footnotes in the New Testament which say if something has been quoted from the Old Testament. Looking back on those Old Testament passages helps us appreciate that all of history is in God's hands, all according to his plan. Now of course, I could enjoy my friend's garden without any reference to the architect's plans, just as you can read any part of Scripture and hear God speak. But there is a richness and depth to God's word which means that there are always more treasures to find, if we will take the time to look.

Wherever we are in the Bible, keeping the focus on Christ is important. The Bible as a whole teaches us that we are saved through Christ alone. Remembering this reduces the danger of plucking a verse out of context and misunderstanding it. For example, we might look at James 1 v 27—"religion that our Father accepts as pure and faultless is this: to look after orphans and widows in their distress and to keep oneself from being polluted by the world"—and conclude that we need to retreat to a monastery and start up an online fund to support widows and orphans before we can be accepted by God. But this can't be the right application when we remember what we know from the whole Bible—for one thing, there is no way to be accepted by God except through Christ. In the context of the book of James, this verse is a warning against claiming to believe in Christ without allowing his love to change the way you live. Which brings us neatly on to…

WHAT DID IT MEAN FOR THE FIRST HEARERS—AND FOR US?

Here's another obvious fact we often miss: each book of the Bible was written by a particular author, at a particular time, addressed to a particular group of people and written for a particular reason.

So before applying a passage to our own context, it's good to try to hear it as if we were the first readers. Think of it like getting inside the air raid shelter and imagining what it would have been like for the people in the Second World War. To do this you need a little background about who the first readers were, and when and where they lived. You can often work this out by reading the beginning and end of the book, although sometimes it may be helpful to use a study Bible and read the introduction in there. There are also really helpful video over-views of each Bible book on the Bible Project's website (thebibleproject.com). Doing this background work will help you to feel the encouragements, reassurances, challenges and shocks as you read as if you were one of the first hearers.

It's also helpful to think about the original author. Why did they write it? What is the main point they are making? (My pastor used to say that "the main things are the plain things and the plain things are the main things".) What's the mood? What's the genre?

Once we have thought about what the text meant for the first hearers, we can answer the question: What does it mean for us? Though written by different authors, the Bible contains the words of one divine author, God. And his words are for us, today. The Bible is one big story which we ourselves are part of; with this is mind, we can see the ways in which what it meant for the first hearers can be applied to us. (The examples in the meditation tool below illustrate what this looks like in practice.)

Helpful questions to ask at this stage are: Is there a command to be obeyed? E.g. "Trust in the LORD with all your heart and lean not on your own understanding" (Proverbs 3 v 5). Is there a promise to believe? E.g. Jesus said, "Surely I am with you always, to the very end of the age" (Matthew 28 v 20). Is there a truth to be remembered? E.g. "Power belongs to you, God, and with you, Lord, is unfailing love" (Psalm 62 v 11-12).

PICK ONE TRUTH

Having searched through the text it is likely that we will have a small pile of treasure: a broken matchbox car, a piece of costume jewellery and hopefully a 10F coin! It is at this point that meditation differs from ordinary Bible study. Next we prayerfully ask God to show us which of these truths he wants us to meditate on. Usually the truth you pick will be the one by which the Spirit has most stirred your heart—perhaps he challenged a particular sin, revealed something new, corrected a wrong way of thinking or reassured you about a troubling situation. Our cry for insight is a prayer God loves to answer—but if you haven't found treasure, ask God. And persevere.

A bit like my brother, sifting through the market stalls looking for the firmest, best tomatoes in order to store them up for winter, we must approach this task with a sense of urgency, knowing how much we need the treasure of God's word. We cannot give up and walk away: "Oh it doesn't matter, I don't really need the truth today". We need to look until we find tomatoes to store up!

In the following chapters we'll walk through how to meditate on the one truth we've chosen.

(Look) MEDITATION TOOL: LOOK

- What do we learn about GOD?
- How do we glimpse CHRIST?
- What did it mean for the FIRST HEARERS, and for US?
- From the truths you've discovered, pick the ONE truth that you will use the following chapters/steps (Turn, Learn, Live) to meditate on.

PUTTING IT INTO PRACTICE
Example 1: Genesis 1

"In the beginning God created the heavens and the earth. Now the earth was formless and empty, darkness was over the surface of the deep, and the Spirit of God was hovering over the waters. And God said, 'Let there be light,' and there was light. God saw that the light was good, and he separated the light from the darkness. God called the light 'day', and the darkness he called 'night'. And there was evening, and there was morning—the first day..." (v 1-5)

- GOD: It's obvious but true—he is the Creator. God is centre stage—and his power is immense enough for him to simply command things into being. There is a sense of order, of beauty, of approval as he looks over creation each day with satisfaction: "It was good" (v 10, 12, 18, 21, 25).
- CHRIST: God is the creator and controller of creation, so when we see Christ calming the storm and walking on water, it makes us ask, could he be God?
- FIRST HEARERS: Humans are created by God.

So they must worship *him*, not the creation (unlike the other nations around Israel at the time).

- US: We are created by God—this is a simple truth, but utterly profound when you think of what that means. We are planned, designed, good. He is in control of us—our past, present and future. We must not worship creation or created things.
- Pick ONE of these truths to use the following steps to meditate on: God is the Creator.

Example 2: Matthew 13 v 31-35

"The kingdom of heaven is like a mustard seed, which a man took and planted in his field. Though it is the smallest of all seeds, yet when it grows, it is the largest of all garden plants and becomes a tree, so that the birds come and perch in its branches…" (v 31-32)

- GOD: It's *his* kingdom. It looks small, but grows to become the largest of all.
- CHRIST: In verse 35 Matthew gives us a quote from Psalm 78 v 2. Jesus is the prophet who reveals things that have been hidden since the creation of the world. So, we need to listen to him, and ask when we don't understand. You may also notice that as the King of this kingdom, Jesus parallels what happens to the kingdom. He appears "small"—just a man dying on a cross—but is raised to glory to become the "largest" King of all.
- FIRST HEARERS: The disciples might have realised the kingdom did look weak and small—just Jesus and a few uneducated fishermen. Hopefully

they were encouraged that it would grow—they had begun to see that happen (Matthew 10) as Jesus sent them out to call people into the kingdom.

- US: As we listen to Jesus explain what the parables mean, we begin to see that his kingdom has grown so much larger—the church is now worldwide, and still growing, and it will continue to grow even when it looks unlikely!
- Pick ONE of these truths to use the following steps to meditate on: God's kingdom starts small but becomes the largest of all.

We'll continue these examples on page 84.

P.S. READING ALOUD

In our culture where we're more used to skimming than reading, digging into the Bible for treasure feels quite alien. Really reading and thinking deeply about what a text says is a skill we may need to learn.

Reading it aloud can help us do this, as it slows us down and makes us think about the meaning of the text. It can also give us a better sense of what sort of literature it is—a letter, a song, a lament or a historical account?

Reading slowly may mean we need to read less—I can personally vouch for the fact that it is hard to mine a large area if you want to dig deep for treasure! I heard the Australian preacher David Cook recommend that for every one minute you read, think about it for four. If time is short, it is better to read less so you can properly think about what it means and how you can live it out.

After all, this is God's word, not an email from our boss, or an article to be devoured before we have to get off the bus. We need to actively reject skim-reading, aware that it is probably our default. The medium we use can really help here too. I would strongly recommend using a real Bible to set it apart from all the other stuff we skim-read on our screens, and to help us to approach it with reverence and to rely on God for insight.

Carefully consider your attitude as you read. Do you really want to find treasure or are you wanting to get this over with so you can get on with doing something "useful"?

CHAPTER 6

Turn Your Heart to Christ

Lord | Look | **Turn** | Learn | Live

Turning your ear to wisdom
and applying your heart to understanding…
Proverbs 2 v 2

In 2005 the Apple CEO, Steve Jobs, gave the commencement address at Stanford University. Here was his parting advice to graduating students:

> And most important, have the courage to follow your heart and intuition. They somehow already know what you truly want to become.

Our culture says that our heart is in the driving seat, and we should follow it.

But Proverbs suggests that in some senses at least, we are in control of our hearts. That's the idea behind Proverbs 2 v 2: "[Make] your ear attentive to wisdom and [incline] your heart to understanding" (ESV).

If we make our ears attentive to God's word, our hearts will incline towards God's wisdom. This is at the heart of biblical meditation. This is where it differs from a "read and pray, shut my Bible and walk away" kind of quiet time. Biblical meditation listens and looks attentively at a truth until it becomes what we treasure.

Proverbs tells us that everything we hear is either one of two voices, which are personified in chapters 7 – 9 as two women: the woman "wisdom", who speaks truth, and the woman "folly", who seduces, persuades and deceives.

To treasure God's wisdom, we don't just look carefully at what he says and all of its benefits—though we definitely do need to do that! We also need to *turn from* the voice of folly.

Let me take you on a shopping trip to Poundland to explain what I mean. In Poundland—as the name suggests—everything is £1. It's full of exciting-looking stuff. The packaging is pretty; the pictures look amazing.

I bought a paddling pool from there once. The picture on the front of the box showed a smiling baby having a fantastic time.

I got it home and opened it up. I kid you not, it was 15cm (6") tall round the edge and 40cm (15.5") wide. It was hardly a paddling pool—it wasn't even a paddling puddle! It was useless—completely unfit for purpose.

I had been *seduced*. I was *persuaded* by the pretty packaging and deceived by the picture of joy on the front. In the shop, my heart wanted it. But when I got it home, the true *consequences* were revealed. Once I had opened it up and exposed what was inside, my heart started to turn—away from the cheap imitation. Now imagine that while I was in the shop I saw another, more beautiful option: an outdoor swimming pool. Crystal-clear blue water. Real, solid, lasting… What would my heart want then?

As we set our hearts on what is real, what is lasting and what really satisfies, we find power to fight the lie that once looked so attractive. We see the promises as empty, the consequences as devastating and the pretty packaging as a lie. We see the paddling puddle for the empty promise it is. And we turn towards the real, lasting, satisfying wisdom of God.

LISTEN ATTENTIVELY - EXPOSE THE LIES

In some ways my paddling puddle was similar to the woman "folly" we meet in Proverbs 7. Here folly is depicted as an "adulterous woman" who is out to seduce a young man passing by. She is way more dangerous than any of the branding execs at Poundland: "With persuasive words she led him astray; she seduced him with her smooth talk" (Proverbs 7 v 21).

She *seduces* the foolish son by appealing to all of his senses as she describes the luxurious feel of her Egyptian cotton bed linen, the decadent colours and the intoxicating smells of the perfumes she has used for her bed (v 16-17).

Three times the extent of her *persuasion* is emphasised in verses 26-27: "Many are the victims she has brought down; her slain are a mighty throng. Her house is a highway to the grave." This is no narrow path that the foolish young man has found himself on, but all four lanes of the M25—a highway to the grave. This is how persuasion often works—by peer pressure. If everyone is doing it, how can it be wrong?

The adulterous woman also deceives the young man about the *consequences* of sin, promising him that they will not get caught: "My husband is not at home; he has gone on a long journey" (v 19). This is a trick the devil often employs—

minimising and removing the consequences, just as he did with Adam and Eve in the garden: "You will not certainly die" (Genesis 3 v 4).

But God doesn't let us remain in our deception. In Proverbs 7 he gives us not one but three disturbing pictures of the consequences. The foolish son is like an ox going to the slaughter, like a deer stepping into a noose and like a bird darting into a snare (v 22-23). The three pictures are followed by three statements: it will cost him his life, he is on a highway to the grave, and it leads down to the chambers of death (ironically literally the bedrooms of death, v 26-27). No wonder Solomon warns his sons, "Do not let your heart turn to her ways or stray into her paths" (v 25).

As we meditate on the "one truth" that we picked at the end of the previous chapter, we can use these three questions to expose the lies we're tempted to believe:

- How does the devil *seduce* us with the opposite of this truth?
- How does the world *persuade* us to respond to this truth?
- What are the *consequences*?

First, look for this in the passage you are studying. For example, this morning I was reading in 1 Kings 18 about Elijah and King Ahab testing who is really God—Baal or the Lord—with a "build two altars and see which god sets theirs on fire" competition. The Lord is proved to be God by miraculously sending fire on his altar, and at the end of the story the people bow down, crying "The LORD—he is

God!" (1 Kings 18 v 39). So that was the truth I was think-ing about—that the Lord is proved to be God time and again throughout Scripture.

So, *how does the devil seduce us with the opposite of the truth?* In the passage Elijah says that the people waver between two opinions, unsure if the Lord is really God or whether the world's gods are better (v 21). Wavering between the Lord and something else is a great description of the devil's seduc-tion. He whispers to us that it's ok to waver—so long as we go to church on Sunday, it doesn't matter how we live the rest of the week.

How does the world persuade us to respond? The world is per-haps more blatant. In the passage Baal had 450 prophets and the Lord had one: Elijah. It must have felt like all Israel fol-lowed Baal! It would have been so hard therefore to genu-inely live for the Lord, who is God.

What are the consequences? In the passage, Israel's worship of Baal had led to trouble, drought, and death. It may look as if it doesn't matter that we go along with worshipping what this world worships—but it does.

LISTEN ATTENTIVELY - EXPLORE THE TRUTH

The next part of the meditation involves examining the beauty of our "one truth" from different angles. As we listen attentively to the truth about God, our hearts will find a greater joy, a stronger pull, a deeper thrill, a lasting satisfac-tion. It's like turning from the paddling puddle to look at the beautifully warm, crystal-clear outdoor swimming pool: the sun glinting off its deep blue waters, the intricately patterned tiles perfectly diffusing the light through the pool, and its calm, warm waters inviting us to refresh ourselves in its pure water. This is what will keep us from straying back to the paddling puddle.

As we consider our one truth, we can use these questions to take time to really explore it so that we see more of how wonderful it is—how real, lasting and satisfying.

- What do we learn about this truth in the passage?
- Where else do we see this truth in Scripture?
- In what ways do we glimpse Christ, his suffering (look for parallels with the consequences of sin) and his glory?

The first place to look is in the passage. What do we learn about this truth: how is it put on display here? Do we see any positive consequences for believing? In what ways is it real, satisfying and lasting?

You could think of how it fits into the wider context of the Bible: where else do we see this truth in Scripture? The more you read your Bible, the more you will begin to see these links where Bible themes are repeated. How is this truth seen in Bible history? How will it be perfectly fulfilled in the new creation? Even if everyone else is thronging in the opposite direction right now, it is God's truth that will last for ever.

Then look for connections between the truth we're considering and Christ's life, death, resurrection and reign from heaven (as he invites us to in Luke 24 v 26-27). It is thrilling to catch a glimpse of these things in places where you would not expect to. The early church father Origen describes this as catching the sound of Jesus' voice from afar and feeling your heart leap in response.

So for example, I was moved this morning as I thought about the consequences of worshipping other gods—trouble, drought and death, and how Jesus suffered each of these at the cross. That punishment was what I deserve for worshipping other gods. Someone died because of my sin—and that "someone" was the perfect Son of God.

TURN YOUR HEART

At a conference last year I heard the American pastor Thabiti Anyabwile preach. Partway through, he turned to us and asked, "How does your heart feel about that truth?"

I was blown away. What a question! What a daring… provocative… *American* thing to ask!

I felt like saying, *Excuse me, but we are British here, and we don't do hearts. Ask me what I think about that. Even ask me what I will do about that. But "how does my heart feel about that?"—that is way above your pay grade!*

But it's actually a very helpful question. Having exposed the lies and explored the truth, we then start to see where our heart is naturally inclining—and seek to turn it towards God. Here are our next steps:

- *Confess how your heart feels about this truth.* Think about the ways in which you are seduced. How hard is it to go against the world when it persuades you to join in?
- *Think about the consequences you deserve and turn to Christ.* What are the consequences of this sin? Do

you really believe that will result? If ever our hearts feel inclined towards sin, we must look at the cross. There we see what sin cost. When we forget and ignore God, when we try to take control and doubt his goodness, we deserve to die. Pause and allow this to soak in. This is the punishment you deserve. Then turn to Jesus and ask him to take the punishment you deserve on himself.

- *Believe that you are forgiven and ask for help to change.* Pause again and consider that Jesus gave himself to redeem you from all wickedness (Titus 2 v 14). No longer will you find yourself seduced, persuaded and deceived. You can change. Jesus doesn't just redeem us—he purifies "for himself a people that are his very own, eager to do what is good" (Titus 2 v 14). Ask God to turn your heart towards this truth, that you might treasure it and be eager to live it out.

TURN YOUR HEART OR YOUR HEART WILL TURN AWAY
The tragedy of Proverbs is that King Solomon—who begged his sons to listen attentively to God so that their hearts would incline towards him—did not heed his own advice. In 1 Kings 11 we find out:

> *King Solomon, however, loved many foreign women ... from nations about which the LORD had told the Israelites, "You must not intermarry with them, because they will surely turn your hearts after their gods." Nevertheless, Solomon held fast to them in*

love. He had seven hundred wives of royal birth and three hundred concubines, and his wives led him astray. As Solomon grew old, his wives turned his heart after other gods, and his heart was not fully devoted to the LORD his God, as the heart of David his father had been. (1 Kings 11 v 1-4)

Solomon taught the importance of turning one's heart towards God, but his own heart treasured women rather than God. He did not turn his heart, so his heart was turned. If we don't turn to Christ by looking at the consequences of our sin and repenting, our hearts will be turned away.

It would be like me, knowing all the problems with the paddling puddle, straying back into Poundland to be seduced by the next glittery shiny bit of packaging.

Solomon knew what he needed to do, but he didn't get rid of the problem—which is why we cannot stop here. We are forgiven—but now we need to make changes to how we live. We need to get out of Poundland! That's where we're going next chapters.

Turn — **MEDITATION TOOL: TURN**

Having picked out ONE truth at the end of the previous step, use the following questions to think about that truth more deeply.

- **Expose the lies**
  How does the devil seduce us with the opposite of this truth?
  How does the world persuade us to respond to this truth?
  What are the consequences?
- **Explore the truth**
  What do we learn about this truth in the passage?
  Where else do we see this truth in Scripture?
  In what ways do we glimpse Christ, his suffering and his glory?
- **Turn your heart**
  Confess how your heart feels about this truth.
  Think about the consequences you deserve and turn to Christ.
  Believe that you are forgiven and ask for help to change.

PUTTING IT INTO PRACTICE

Example 1: Genesis 1

Truth: *God is the Creator.*

Expose the lies

- *The devil:* He seduces us into thinking we can be in control, and that God is not really in control, or not working for our good. For example, how can he be in control when I haven't found a husband yet? It may be better to take control and see if it works out with that guy from the office...

■ *Our world:* People dismiss the notion that God is the Creator. It feels like everyone believes this world evolved from nothing rather than being a beautiful, ordered and carefully designed reflection of our beautiful God.

■ *Consequences:* Does it matter whether our world was created by God or the result of a random big bang? We only need to read on into Genesis 3 to see the consequences of rejecting God's rule: death.

Explore the truth

■ *In the passage:* God creates a good, ordered, fruitful, blessed creation.

■ *Scripture:* Throughout Scripture God is always in control. We read in Acts 2 that even at the darkest point in history, the men who crucified Jesus were acting according to God's deliberate plan and foreknowledge. Right now God is sitting on his throne in heaven—everything is under his control and one day he will make everything right. It is good and right to long for this day.

■ *Christ:* He displayed his authority over creation as he stilled the storm and healed sickness. He has authority over everything in my life and will give me all I need (including the relationships I need) to serve him.

Turn your heart

If I'm honest, I often doubt that God is in control, and I fail to believe that people are really in danger of his wrath. I do try to live as if I am the creator—I act as though I am limitless when I try to be everything and do everything.

Lord, I am exhausted. I admit that I am weak and limited and that you are the Creator. I'm sorry Jesus had to suffer for my mutiny. Please forgive me for wanting to take your place. Please help me to love being the created one, reliant on you to enable me to look after your creation.

Example 2: Matthew 13 v 31-32

Truth: *God's kingdom starts small but becomes the largest of all.*

Expose the lies

- *The devil:* He seduces us into thinking that he is the powerful, lasting king.
- *The world:* The world seeks to persuade us that the kingdoms of this world are the places to invest our lives in, not God's kingdom. They are the powerful kingdoms.
- *Consequences:* Read on in the passage—a few verses later we see that God weeds all evildoers out of his kingdom and throws them into the blazing furnace.

Explore the truth

- *In the passage:* God's kingdom does grow, it is powerful, it will become the largest, strongest kingdom, and it will endure for ever.
- *Scripture:* You could think about the different ways that God's kingdom appears weak but grows

anyway. For example, Jesus built his church on the foundation of twelve uneducated fishermen, yet 2,000 years later it is still growing! Heaven is described as a vast multitude that no one can count, from every nation, tribe, people and language. This is what the small mustard seed grows into!

- *Christ:* On the cross, one man died in weakness. Yet out of this apparently weak and small seed many, many, many people are forgiven and made righteous and brought into God's kingdom.

Turn your heart

I realise from exploring this that my heart does believe that this world is the most powerful place to invest my time in, and I am embarrassed to tell people of God's kingdom because it seems so small and weak.

Lord, I'm sorry for getting it so wrong. I'm sorry that Jesus suffered the blazing furnace of your anger in my place. Please forgive me. I am so excited by the description in Revelation 7, where your kingdom gets so large that there is a multitude from every people group. That is really amazing. Please help me to tell my family and friends about Jesus so they can be safe in the only kingdom that lasts.

P.S. FIVE WAYS TO FIGHT DISTRACTION

I was sitting among the students at church recently, and noticed that a number of them were distracted by their phones during the prayers and communion. I despaired at the younger generation! Then I reached into my bag and checked the time on my phone. And then I saw that one of the church staff had messaged me. And then I replied… in the middle of the sermon!

My hypocrisy was bad, but what mortified me was that the text captured my folly on record!

Even in Solomon's day, he felt the need to command people to be attentive (Proverbs 2 v 2). Here are some ways to prick up our ears and fight distraction as we come to God's word:

1. Choose a time when you are alert. Puritan preacher John Owen says this of reading God's word: "If we will allow only the refuse of our time unto this duty, [when we] are fit for nothing else, we are not to expect any great success in it … Therefore … choose the seasons for it wherein you are most fit" (*The Grace and Duty of Being Spiritually Minded*, p. 131).

2. Choose a quiet place and cut out distractions. Put your phone in another room and use a real Bible. If you need to keep track of time, get a watch!

3. Before you begin, quieten your mind by focusing on your breathing for a few breaths. This

is a tool used in secular meditation to calm the distracted mind. Breathe in for as long as it takes to read this sentence… breathe out for as long as it takes to read this sentence… You could write down the distracting thoughts so that you don't need to keep hold of them while you read.

4. Write down what you think about the passage, to help you articulate, consolidate and remember. Or think and pray out loud.

5. Train your brain. When you get distracted, just direct your thoughts back to what you should be doing. When I first started using the "Lord, Look, Turn, Learn, Live" meditation technique, I set a timer for each section, so as to limit any daydreaming to a maximum of five minutes! After a while you won't need the timer and will find it easier to concentrate.

Above all, ask God to help you to listen attentively. He is the God of miracles after all!

CHAPTER 7

Learn the Truth

Lord | Look | Turn | **Learn** | Live

Store up my commands within you...
Proverbs 2 v 1

At school I invested quite a bit of time learning trigonometry, and it has stayed with me for nearly thirty years. I can remember not just the acronym SOHCAHTOA, but what it actually means (sine = opposite / hypotenuse, cosine = adjacent / hypotenuse, tangent = opposite / adjacent).

I used that knowledge for the first time a few weeks ago! Well... I used it to help my son learn it for his exams. Now he too is thoroughly prepared in case he should need to work out the length of the sides of a right-angle triangle at any point in the next 30 years.

How is it that many of us were prepared to invest our efforts into learning such pointless, useless information for the sake of a qualification; yet we rarely think to invest any effort into learning the precious words of life spoken by the great God of the universe?

But it's not just the hard work involved that stops us memorising Scripture. We're also out of practice. At a quiz night recently, banned from reaching for my phone, I realised that I hardly ever use my memory—I just look on the internet!

We've reached step four in our meditation tool. So far we've prayed ("Lord"), read the Bible ("Look"), and thought about what it means ("Turn"). We so often walk away from Bible reading at this point, content to have understood and been forgiven. But God wants to go deeper—to "store up" or, more literally, "treasure up" this truth within us (v 1). God commands us to dig out that little-used capacity, the memory, dust it off and put it to work.

Why? Because like my brother storing up tomatoes for the winter, we need to store up God's truth within us so that we can access it when we need it. That's why memorising God's word is so integral to the vitality of our walk with the Lord. Seven times in six chapters of Proverbs we are given similar instructions: we are told to store up God's commands within us; to write them on the tablet of our hearts; bind them on our fingers and round our necks; to keep them within our hearts (Proverbs 2 v 1, 3 v 1, 3 v 3, 4 v 21, 6 v 21, 7 v 1, 7 v 3).

And God's word itself gives us some ideas how.

MEMORY AIDS

Fix these words of mine in your hearts and minds, tie them as symbols on your hands and bind them on your foreheads. Teach them to your children, talking about them when you sit at home and when you walk along the road, when you lie down and when you get up. Write them on the door-frames of your houses and on your gates. (Deuteronomy 11 v 18-20)

Although Arthur Fry holds the patent for inventing the Post-it Note in 1974, you could argue that the idea traces way back to Moses' day. God commanded his people to decorate their doorframes, gates, clothing and body parts with Scripture to help them remember it and therefore live it out.

So writing a Bible verse on your hand is right up there in Deuteronomy 6! I'm sure if they'd had smartphones, God would also have suggested photographing the verse and setting it as their wallpaper, texting themselves the verse, and setting reminders in their schedules.

I have a very peculiar habit of wearing elastic bands on my wrists. When I had post-natal depression I was struggling with negative thoughts obsessively going around my head. So I would write a Bible truth on the band, then every time I had a negative thought I would swap it to the other wrist and ask God to forgive me and help me to think truth. It must have looked quite weird, but it was also quite biblical (the memory aid bit—not specifically the elastic bands!).

Numbers 15 v 38-39 develops this idea of fixing God's words in our hearts and minds:

> *Throughout the generations to come you are to make tassels on the corners of your garments, with a blue cord on each tassel. You will have these tassels to look at and so you will remember all the commands of the LORD, that you may obey them.*

Throughout the following chapters, we also find descriptions of some less palatable memory aids. A group of 250 Israelites from the tribe of Levi rebel against Moses and

Aaron's leadership—and as a result, God destroys them with fire. Among their charred remains are the metal censers they had used to burn incense. God instructs Moses to have the censers hammered into sheets to overlay the altar, to remind the Israelites of the consequences of sin. A short time later, when the Israelites question Aaron's authority to lead them, God tells Moses to collect the staffs of the leaders of the twelve tribes, and says that whoever's staff sprouts is God's chosen leader. Aaron's staff not only buds, but blossoms and produces almonds! It is left in front of the ark as a sign to the rebellious to put an end to their grumbling.

Sadly, it does not work. Memory aids only help people who want to change. By the time we get to Matthew 23, the Pharisees have taken the command of Deuteronomy to new, extreme proportions. They have supersized the boxes containing Scripture verses that are worn on the forehead and arm: "They make their phylacteries wide and the tassels on their garment long," says Jesus (v 5). Why? Because "everything they do is done for people to see" (v 5)—so the more prominent the better, however bizarre. They must have looked ridiculous. But Jesus isn't laughing. Instead he pronounces woe on their hypocritical religion, saying that these Pharisees are like whitewashed tombs, which look beautiful on the outside but on the inside are full of the bones of the dead. The very thing that they fear—something unclean which would defile them if they touched it—is actually inside of them.

Scripture memory is important as a tool, but we must beware making it an end in itself. We are not aiming to memorise the Bible so that we can fill up a sticker chart, give ourselves a pat on the back, or feel quietly smug in a Bible study. This will be of no benefit. Proverbs 2 does not say, "Memorise God's word, then you will feel good and impress people". It says, "Treasure up my commandments within you … then you will understand the fear of the LORD and find the knowledge of God" (Proverbs 2 v 1, 5, ESV).

My husband had to learn the periodic table for his Chemistry degree. He didn't treasure it up. It was information. However, when he learned our wedding vows, that was different. Those words define our life together. They were worth learning, and worth displaying on our bedroom wall to this day.

Certain sections of the Bible are actually written in a format designed to be memorised, using a device called an acrostic, where each line begins with successive letters of the alphabet. It's hard to recognise in our Bibles, as the acrostic element doesn't translate from Hebrew into English. But the footnotes tell us that Lamentations 1 – 4, Proverbs 31 v 10-31 and Psalms 25, 34, 37, 111, 112, 119 and 145 are all written as acrostics. They were intended to be memorable. It is biblical to think of ways to make God's word memorable—whether that's drawing a mind map, devising an acronym to help you remember successive ideas, or simply repeating a verse over and over again to ourselves. And it's right to expect this to take some hard work (much like writing an acrostic would!).

It's worth the work because being able to recall a text to help you fight the battle for holiness or make hard decisions or give counsel to others is actually profoundly useful. Make sure that your heart doesn't just have leftover exam revision written in it. Make the effort to store something life changing in there!

SINGING

Meditation is inextricably linked with singing. Almost all of the verses which mention meditation are psalms—i.e. songs (to be sung!). Why? Because songs have a way of getting stuck in our heads! And as we sing them to ourselves (and others) we meditate on the words. It's not just psalms that we can sing. Paul writes in Colossians 3 v 16: "Let the message of Christ dwell among you richly as you teach and admonish one another with all wisdom through psalms, hymns and songs from the spirit, singing to God with gratitude in your hearts".

On every holiday since our kids were young, our family has committed Scripture to memory using song. It started with the Lord's Prayer and some memory verse songs by the children's entertainer Colin Buchanan. We then got a bit more creative, and I started asking God to help me put psalms to a tune so that we could learn them. We now have a collection of about 20 psalms, which we sing and talk about on Sundays as a way of making sure we keep on remembering them rather than it being a one-off.

It feels pretty insignificant most of the time, learning these truths to silly tunes (like the theme tune to the kids' TV show *Octonauts*). But over the years there have been many precious times when we have been under pressure and recalling these verses enabled us to hold fast to God in the struggle.

Take, for example, the camping holiday that almost ended in disaster when 40mph winds struck the idyllic viewpoint upon which we had pitched our tent (on my insistence), snapping poles and ripping the fabric. As my husband Jonty fled to a camping shop for equipment to fix it, I tried to take the tent down (at which point it turned into a parachute). My youngest son started singing the psalm we had been learning as a family, and suggested we pray to God for help, since what we had been learning was: "God is our refuge and strength, an ever-present help in trouble. Therefore we will not fear, though the earth give way!" (Psalm 46 v 1-2).

Out of the mouth of babes…

But bless him, his was the right response. His words stopped me in my tracks, and we did indeed huddle and pray that God would be our ever-present help. It was quite striking looking back! God did miraculously help us to get the tent down, and find a new place to camp—an empty spot at the back of the campsite surrounded on three sides with mini cliffs, completely sheltered from the gale. By the time Jonty arrived back a neighbouring family had leant us everything we needed to fix the tent, we had got it all moved and fully erected and were sat relaxing in this sheltered little sun trap! God was our refuge and help. He was our ever-present help in trouble. I just hadn't believed that those verses really applied to me. But my son did. And he had those words at his disposal because they'd been written on his heart through song.

At other times these "vacation psalm songs" have spurred us on to obedience, or given voice to truth in moments of deep sadness, or have helped us to delight in God more than we delight in this world. We learned Psalm 63 together when my parents took us to Disney World. As we walked past the "happiest place on earth" sign, we were able to respond in the words of Psalm 63: "Because your love is better than life [and Disney], my lips will glorify you [not Disney]".

You don't need to be a musical genius to do this. Just pick a verse from your Bible time and make up a little tune, or put the words to a tune you know already. Then just keep singing it to yourself throughout your day. As long as it's helping you meditate, it doesn't really matter how it sounds. Or you could use resources that are already out there. There are many great hymns and songs based on Scripture.

Singing is not just God's gift to us for now, but for eternity. In heaven we will be singing. And do you know what we will be singing? Scripture! In Revelation 15 v 3-4 a crowd of believers sing "the song of God's servant Moses and of the Lamb". They're words drawn from Psalm 111, 86, 98, Deuteronomy 32 and Jeremiah 10.

We're going to spend an eternity singing the words of God. So let's get practising now!

TALKING

A third important way of remembering, which God commands his people to exercise in Deuteronomy 6 and 11, is to *talk* about the commands:

> *These commandments that I give you today are to be on your hearts. Impress them on your children. Talk about them when you sit at home and when you walk along the road, when you lie down and when you get up. (Deuteronomy 6 v 6-7)*

Remember back to our introductory definition of meditation—talking to yourself in your heart. Biblical meditation is talking to yourself about God's commands. It's only natural that this will overflow into talking to other people about them. As Jesus said, "The mouth speaks what the heart is full of" (Matthew 12 v 34).

Think for a moment about what you talk about, and you'll soon realise that you talk about what you think about. If you're thinking about how pleased you are with that bargain you picked up in the supermarket, you will share that as you walk along the road with your friend. If you are really gutted that your football team lost at the weekend, you'll have a rant about it with your neighbour when you bump into them. If you're shivering as you wait for the bus, you'll randomly start up a conversation with the person next to you about how it is unseasonably cold for June (ok, maybe we wouldn't all do that...).

So if we are not talking much about God as we walk along the street, get up, lie down, sit at our desks, share a cup of tea after church, chat before the prayer meeting... could that be because his words are not written on our hearts? Too often we have shut our Bibles in the morning, walked away and forgotten what we have learned.

A friend recently told me that in his home church there was a culture of talking about the sermon after the service. Everyone just did it, and there were questions on the screen afterwards to help. How did that culture start? It simply started with one person determined to talk about what God had been saying to them. Could you be that one?

As we treasure God's truth and are more excited about it (because we're using the tools from the previous chapters), we'll want to talk about it. And this is a kind of virtuous circle: as we talk about it, we'll get more excited about it. We'll remind ourselves of it all over again. And we'll help the people we're talking to about it be more excited too—and then they can speak truth back to us.

Why not give it a go? Start a conversation. During your quiet time you could think and pray through your day and ask God to give you opportunities to share his truth with others. There have been times when I've prayed specifically before visiting a neighbour, that God would keep a truth at the forefront of my mind so that I could talk about it if I got an opportunity. Maybe you're going to some kind of social event later, and you could think of how to turn the conversation around to a related topic in the hope of being able to share the truth. Expect and ask God to give you an opportunity to start a conversation about this truth.

(Learn) **MEDITATION TOOL: LEARN**

Pick a verse or symbol to help you remember this truth. Pray and plan how you will write this truth on your heart—through memory aids, singing, talking to yourself and others about it.

PUTTING IT INTO PRACTICE
Example 1: Genesis 1
Truth: *God is Creator.*

- *Memory aids:* You could memorise the phrase "In the beginning God…" Maybe photograph that Bible verse and set it as your wallpaper, or text the verse to yourself.

- *Singing:* "O Lord my God, when I in awesome wonder consider all the works thy hand hath made … Then sings my soul … How great thou art!" What a great song that would be to have ringing through your ears as you go into your day.

- *Talk about it in your heart and to others:* As you go through your day, spend a few moments thinking about what you learned and praising God for that truth. It might be that you notice yourself sinning in one of the ways you confessed this morning. Take a moment to recall the verse and ask for forgiveness and the Holy Spirit's help to love the truth. You could set a reminder with that verse to pop up on your phone on your lunchbreak or at dinnertime, to remind you to pray, think and talk about it over your meal.

Example 2: Matthew 13 v 31-35

Truth: *God's kingdom starts small but becomes the largest of all*

- *Memory aids:* You could simply put a dot on your hand with a biro to remind you of how small a mustard seed starts off. When you notice it, remind yourself that however small God's kingdom seems—and however large the kingdoms of the world seem—God's kingdom will be the largest.

- *Singing:* "Your kingdom come, your will be done" is a great way to respond to this verse (Matthew 6 v 10) to help you long for the day when everyone will see God's kingdom for what it truly is. You could listen to the song "Let Your Kingdom Come" by Sovereign Grace Music.

- *Talk about it in your heart and to others:* It would be interesting to start a conversation with others about kingdoms. The only thing that every kingdom (or government, or business, or celebrity) has in common is that it rises and then it falls. It would not be difficult then to mention that "the Bible talks about a kingdom that is very different—one built on something apparently weak and small, yet growing larger by the day".

P.S. THE WRITING ON MY HEART

A friend of mine was badly bullied at high school. To this day she continues to wake up with the repeated mantra "fat, ugly, worthless" reverberating in her ears.

All of us will have words from the past written upon our hearts. Often those words define much of who we are and how we live, even in ways we don't realise.

1 Peter 1 v 18 tells us that we have been "redeemed from the empty way of life handed down to [us] … with the precious blood of Christ". We are redeemed—set free. The scars from our past remain, but we can begin to rewrite those words with new words of life.

It's a battle. But God's words have power to keep on redeeming. So, as she wakes up, my friend can answer those bullies back. "You knit me together in my mother's womb" or "I am fearfully and wonderfully made" or "I am worth more than many sparrows". That is the truth.

Sometimes we need to make the space and time to go down deeper into our motives ("Why did I react like that?") and further back in our personal history ("When have I felt like this before? Who has done that to me before? What do I believe as a result?") to see what time has written on our hearts. Then we can use meditation to begin to unlearn what is not true, and replace it with God's truth.

FEED DAY AND NIGHT

Introduction

"… then you will understand the fear of the LORD
and find the knowledge of God."
Proverbs 2 v 5

When the father in Proverbs 2 commands his son to "accept his words" (v 1), he doesn't just want his son to *listen*—he wants him to live it out. This is made obvious by the verses that follow. As God speaks, he is "a shield" in times of trouble (v 7); he "guards the course" and "protects the way" of his people (v 8); he enables them to "understand what is right and just and fair—every good path" (v 9). God's words are to become part of us and inform every decision we make. Wisdom is seen in how we walk.

Or think of it this way. Remember my brother storing up those tomatoes? Why bother to sterilise all those Kilner jars, lug the tomatoes back from the market, carefully sort through them to root out the bad ones, then wash and chop the good ones? Why bother carefully cooking them to the correct temperature and seasoning them, before decanting them endlessly into narrow-necked jars?

It would have been weird to have gone to all that effort just to create a nice display in his kitchen. So why bother? Because winter was coming.

WINTER FUEL

It's "winter" out in our world! No one is living according to God's word; everyone is going in the opposite direction. This side of Jesus' return, we're walking through the wasteland, with temptation and suffering buffeting us like a headwind. When we don't have God's word open in front of us, the cold starts to bite.

The situation feels more desolate when you consider that even King Solomon—the wisest man in all the earth—could not heed his own advice. He listened to the words, and learned them, but they did not become such a part of him that they informed every decision he made.

So what hope do we have of taking God's words and keeping going with them through the winter?

In ourselves we have no hope.

But then we look at Christ and we have every hope.

For in Christ, we meet a greater, stronger, wiser King. A King who endured the darkest winter: "For the joy that was set before him he endured the cross, scorning its shame" (Hebrews 12 v 2).

What was it that sustained him through the winter? It was the Scriptures. The words of Psalm 119 v 11—"I have hidden your word in my heart that I might not sin against you"—describe what we see on every page of Jesus' life. As he was led into temptation in the desert, he fought the tempter with the words of Scripture hidden in his heart (Luke 4 v 1-13). When confronted with the Pharisees' hypocrisy, he rebuked them with the words of Isaiah: "These people honour me with their lips, but their hearts are far from me" (Mark 7 v 6). When he was tested about the greatest commandment, he showed that the desire to love God with all his being was hidden in his heart from Deuteronomy 6: "'Love the Lord your God with all your heart and with all your soul and with all your mind.' This is the first and greatest commandment" (Matthew 22 v 37-38). Through the distress of his crucifixion he quoted Psalm 22: "My God, my God, why have you forsaken me?" (Matthew 27 v 46). It was as if he bled Scripture. In him we see an echo of Psalm 119 v 23: "Though rulers sit together and slander me, your servant will meditate on your decrees".

And the beautiful thing is that Christ's perfect life and perfect obedience—that perfect meditation that enabled him to endure the dark winter of the cross—is our hope. He did it for us because, on our own, we don't obey and we can't obey.

In the depths of winter, our confidence is not that we can meditate but that he perfectly did. As we come to Christ we find not only the grace that forgives but the power to take those words and live them out.

FEED ON HIM

Christ's victory does not mean we can dive under the duvet and wait it out until summer. No, we have the responsibility of setting our hearts and minds on him:

> Since, then, you have been raised with Christ, set your hearts on things above, where Christ is, seated at the right hand of God. Set your minds on things above, not on earthly things. For you died, and your life is now hidden with Christ in God. When Christ,

who is your life, appears, then you also will appear with him in glory. (Colossians 3 v 1-3)

We need to keep feeding on him so that we keep going through the winter until Christ returns and we see him face to face! Just as my brother stored up tomatoes so that he could eat them later, so too we "store up" God's truth in our hearts (as per section 2) so that we can feed on it and live it out, day and night, as we go about our business in this wintry world.

Looking at all of the Bible verses that mention meditation, they fit broadly into three categories: meditation helps us delight in God's word, obey God's word and hold fast to God's word. This dovetails with God's summary of living out the truth in Deuteronomy 11 v 22: "To love the LORD your God, to walk in obedience to him and to hold fast to him". In the final three chapters, we are going to take these three concepts—delight, obey, hold fast—to explore how meditating on Christ helps us to LIVE out the truth through the winter of this world.

Live out the truth

Obey

Delight

Hold
Fast

Live

Lord

Turn

Learn

Look

Store up the truth

CHAPTER 8

Meditation Awakens our Delight

We think about the things we love. We've all witnessed the truth of this. When two people are falling in love, they are constantly thinking of one another. They daydream about their beloved. They smile as they walk past their beloved's favourite bakery or spot in the park. As they decide what to wear before a date, they wonder whether or not he or she will like it. Their lover is the soundtrack that occupies their mind. All day long, their thoughts are drawn to the one they love.

This is how the psalmist feels in Psalm 119. But not about another human. He feels this way about God's law:

> *Oh, how I love your law!*
> *I meditate on it all day long. (Psalm 119 v 97)*

He doesn't just *like* God's law. Over 176 verses of this psalm, it's as if he runs out of words to convey the depth of his love for God's law—the word in verse 97 literally means he breathes after it. The psalmist longs for God's law, pants after it, meditates on it... Why? Because he loves God. The psalmist is not reading a rulebook in bed every night because he just loves rules. The psalmist loves God's law because through it (as we saw in chapter 4) he can know this great God and fear him rightly.

My problem is that I don't love God like that. And I'm guessing you probably don't either. If we think about what we love, then what I love is food and me-time (whether that is my next holiday or simply a glass of wine on the sofa once the kids have gone to bed). Maybe for you it's the thought of being in a relationship, getting a promotion, watching a box set, opening a cool beer, or even just crawling into bed. These are the places our minds go to, to get us through the day.

Although they didn't have the joys of box sets or flights abroad in 17th-century Britain, the preacher Edmund Calamy similarly observed:

> Love is a loadstone [magnet] of meditation; and he that loves good things will think of them: ... A man that is deep in love with a woman, you need not bid him think of that woman. Where the love is, there the soul is. Oh, did you delight in the things of heaven, I need not lay down rules to persuade you to the practise of it; the very love would be a loadstone. (*The Art of Divine Meditation*, p 153-154)

Where the thoughts are, there the love is. Where the love is, there the soul is. So it's a bit chicken and egg... I don't love God like the psalmist, so I don't meditate on him at all, let alone think about him all day long. But because I don't meditate on him, my love for him is not growing; in fact, it will be going cold.

I know I'm not the only one who struggles with this because in a recent survey at our church, when asked what is hardest about moving forwards as a Christian, over half of people replied, "Spending time with God". The most common reasons people gave for not reading the Bible were not wanting to, forgetting to, and then feeling guilty because they hadn't made it a priority.

Does that resonate with you? We *believe* that God is delightful but we just don't *feel* it. We want to want to meditate on him, but when we don't feel delight, it's hard to get going.

So what should we do?

In ourselves we have no hope. But in Christ, we have every hope. As we come to him, we find the grace that forgives and the power to delight in the relationship he has won for us with our Father in heaven. In Christ we *can* delight; but sometimes that takes discipline.

DISCIPLINE LEADS TO DELIGHT

My husband, Jonty, and I have just celebrated our 20th wedding anniversary. We're way past the dreamy falling in love phase. But we do want to continue to delight in our relationship. And if there's one thing I've learned in 20 years of marriage, it's this: delight takes discipline.

For Jonty and I that looks like planning time each week to go out for a leisurely breakfast: Friday morning, 10 a.m. We talk, discuss Sunday's sermon and pray together.

Without the discipline of that fixed point in our schedule we could easily go a whole week without properly talking! Does the fact that I have Jonty in my diary mean romance is dead or that the delight is gone? No. I have him in my diary precisely *because* I want to delight in him. Our delight grows as we spend time together. And then because the time is delightful, in between our "dates" I find myself thinking of him more, texting him, phoning him—not because I need to but just to say "Hi". I look forward to the next time. Discipline and delight go hand in hand.

The psalmist's delight in God went hand in hand with discipline too. He deliberately learned God's law: "I have hidden your word in my heart, that I might not sin against you" (v 11); "With my lips I recount all the laws that come from your mouth" (v 13).

Nor did he utter Psalm 119 itself as a spontaneous outburst of delight in God—he disciplined himself to write it as an acrostic poem, the stanzas of which begin with successive letters of the Hebrew alphabet; moreover, the verses of each stanza begin with the same letter of the Hebrew alphabet. (We can't see this in our English Bibles because the translation from Hebrew to English obscures it.) The psalmist disciplined himself to arrange the words and sentiments in a way that makes it easier to remember. And he wrote down Psalm 119, so that we can do the same.

Did that mean romance was dead for the psalmist? Not at all: "Oh how I love your law, I meditate on it all day long!" (v 97). But the discipline of learning God's law and the delight in the One who inspired it went hand in hand.

Our delight will grow as we discipline ourselves to learn God's word. But we mustn't wait until we want to do it. We need to get the diary out and put time with God in it! This is why section 2 was so important. We need to set aside time to read God's word in such a way as to write it on our hearts, so that we can take it with us into our day. As we write the truth on our heart, we can meditate on it "when [we] sit at home and when [we] walk along the road, when [we] lie down and when [we] get up" (Deuteronomy 6 v 7). In this way our "quiet time" expands to fill our whole day, our whole lives.

Imagine your day as a page in a book. The "text" is the work we have to do, the people we need to meet, the endless to-do list. But there is always white space around the edges—and often more than we think there is (since on average people spend 2 hours, 22 minutes per day on social media and messaging platforms!5).

Just as lovers spend that white space around the edges thinking of one another, so we can use that white space around the edges to delight in God. At first, we will have to discipline ourselves to do it—our minds will naturally default to the old autopilot habits. But these habits can be broken. We can form new habits which turn our minds to think of what we have been learning of God.

That's where the ideas in chapter 7—Learn—come in. Later in the day we can glance at the note on our hand or in our phone, or recall the song we were singing, or recap the verse we learned. As we discipline ourselves to meditate on God's truth, we will find our delight in God growing. It

IS chicken and egg. The more we delight in God, the more we will find our thoughts and hearts tuning in to what he is saying; and the more we will have to say to him in return…

Delighting in God's truth won't just fuel our Bible reading; it will also fuel our prayers. In Psalm 39 David is angry at the wicked people around him but resolves to keep his mouth shut (v 1-2). The tension builds through the first couple of verses, and then we arrive at verse 3: "While I meditated, the fire burned; then I spoke with my tongue…" Yet the words that follow are not a tirade at his enemy but an explosion of passionate prayer to the Lord (v 4-13). Meditation will likewise move us to pray. As we go about our day, we not only talk to *ourselves* about God's truth, but talk to *God* about God's truth! And as we speak to him, our delight in him grows.

Decide now how you want to start. Perhaps you could plan to have breakfast each week with God? Why not actually write it into your schedule now as a fixed event? Begin your "breakfast" by crying out to the Lord. Look for truth, turn from the lies, learn the truth. Then look ahead into your day and plan how you could keep coming back to feed on it. Are there spaces where you could be delighting in that truth? You may find it helpful to set an alarm, to re-train you in this new habit.

I have found writing something symbolic on my hand helpful (today it's the word "secret", which reminds me of my memory verse, 2 Kings 17 v 9). People will often ask me what is written on my hand, which opens up great opportunities! It's very easy to say: "Well I was reading in my

Bible this morning…" During the devotional time it can be helpful to plan and pray for such opportunities, and to ask, "How would I explain this truth to an unbeliever?"

"But I don't have time for all this!" I hear you cry. Lovers don't try to *find* time to spend together, they *make* time to be together. Put God in your diary first and you will find the rest of life falls into place. But it's also about making better use of our time. Instead of wasting the white space, use it to meditate on truth.

TUNING INTO THE SOUNDTRACK OF CREATION

Delight and discipline go hand in hand, but God is not passively waiting for us to do all the hard work as we open his word. He is constantly speaking to us through another book: "the volumes of creation", as puritan writer Richard Baxter called it (*The Saints' Everlasting Rest*, p 183).

Psalm 19 records a "meditation of [David's] heart" (v 14). It is God, not David, who starts the conversation, by speaking to him through creation:

> *The heavens declare the glory of God;*
> *   the skies proclaim the work of his hands.*
> *Day after day they pour forth speech;*
> *   night after night they reveal knowledge.*
> *They have no speech, they use no words;*
> *   no sound is heard from them.*
> *Yet their voice goes out into all the earth,*
> *   their words to the ends of the world.*
> *(Psalm 19 v 1-4)*

Imagine David, navigating the text of his day. In a moment of "white space" he looks up at the skies. As he looks, he begins to hear their "voice" declaring, proclaiming, revealing to him that there is a glorious God who is working in all the earth (v 1-2). The creation is God's masterpiece. Like any stunning piece of art, creation speaks. So David begins to meditate: *Who made this? Who is responsible for such beauty, intricacy, power? Who can I thank?*

As God uses creation to lift up his eyes, David is reminded of where this voice is most clearly and distinctly heard—through God's word. In the second part of the psalm he turns to worship God for how precious and sweet his fuller revelation is in his word: "[Your decrees] are more precious than gold, than much pure gold; they are sweeter than honey, than honey from the honeycomb" (Psalm 19 v 10).

God is constantly calling to us in the white space around the edges of our day—he is speaking, proclaiming and revealing himself to us through his creation. Wherever we are, we can lift our ears from the soundtracks of the world to tune into his perfect soundtrack.

Even though I live in a big city, I can still see little bits of God's creation that lift my eyes from my temporary lovers up to the true Lover of my soul. And as I am reminded of him, then I can remind myself of the truths I am learning about him. Like David, hearing God's voice in creation prompts me to recall God's voice from his word. I can look down on my hand to see what I learned that morning or think back to Sunday's sermon and delight again in the truths he is teaching me.

One of the most attractive parts of mindfulness is the idea of being fully present in one's surroundings by taking notice of what you can see, hear and feel: hear the birdsong, see the perfect white of the lily contrasting with its deep green stem, feel the cool rain. The Bible doesn't talk about "being present", but it does talk about waking up. The message of Psalm 19 is, essentially, *Wake up and smell the roses!* God intends for creation to snap us out of autopilot so that we can see who he is, and by extension, who we are.

Wherever you are right now, why not look out of the window and listen to what the heavens are saying to you? Respond with a simple prayer of praise to our great God.

REWRITING THE SOUNDTRACKS OF THE WORLD

Like Psalm 19, Psalm 104 records what is described by the psalmist as "[his] meditation" (Psalm 104 v 34). It too is a meditation on God's creation, inviting us to delight in God through what we hear and see in the world around us. But as we dig deeper, there is even more to see.

At the time when the psalms were written, ancient Egypt was the pre-eminent civilisation. So it's interesting that Psalm 104 bears striking resemblances to a song that the Egyptians used to worship their sun god, called *The Great Hymn to the Aten* (you can find an English translation online[6]).

The Bible commentator Derek Kidner writes that Psalm 104 "displays the incalculable difference between worshipping the sun and worshipping its Maker; indeed the psalm's apparent allusions to this famous hymn [to the Aten] seem designed to call attention to this very point" (*Psalms 73 – 150*, p 401).

It's as if the psalmist has taken the soundtrack that his world sings and rewritten it with the truth. He is "answering back" to the soundtrack of his world: *No, the sun god did not set the earth on its foundations—the Lord MY God did. He is very great. He is clothed in majesty and splendour. Yahweh brings forth food from the earth, not the sun god.*

We see from Psalm 104 that part of meditation is thinking critically about whatever messages come our way, rather than just passively absorbing them. Meditation is digging deep into those messages to understand what they are saying, identifying the "itch", and comparing that to God's truth.

We can meditate in this way any time we watch TV or listen to a podcast or scroll past ads online. I recently saw an ad for a film with the line, "The answers we seek are just outside of our reach". And I thought to myself, "No, they are not! God has stepped into our world to give us the answers we need." And as I thought about that wonderful truth, I praised God for it!

Or as an unbelieving family member sends yet another awesome picture of his cruise around Greenland, why not respond gently with, "Wow—it's hard to look at that and not wonder whether there might be a God"? I did that once with my parents. It sparked an amazing conversation, and ended up with me texting them Romans 1 v 20: "Since the creation of the world God's invisible qualities—his eternal power and divine nature—have been clearly seen, being understood from what has been made, so that people are without excuse". (I then had a little panicked prayer in case I had overstepped a line, but they responded to say that the waiter on their cruise had also given them a Bible verse and it was also from Romans!) God speaks through his creation, and it's an easy book to open with our unbelieving family and friends.

Think of a recent TV show, book or film you have seen. Meditate—dig. What is the underlying message? How does it compare to God's message of truth? Plan a conversation starter and ask God for an opportunity to talk to someone specific about it.

Delight is not something that you can keep to yourself. Discipline yourself to delight in God's word, then let it over-flow to others in your life.

Delight   MEDITATION TOOL: DELIGHT

Look ahead into your day. Are there spaces where you could delight in Christ? Meditate on creation? Think critically about the world's soundtracks? Explore what you've learned with others?

CHAPTER 9

The Fruit of Obedience Grows from the Root of Meditation

I have a good friend who was converted as a child from a difficult home background around 20 years ago. When I met up with her recently, she was bubbling over with excitement about a talk she'd heard about the human heart. "For 20 years," she said, "I've been working on my mouth. The problem isn't my mouth, it's my heart! I've been working on the wrong thing!"

For two decades, she had been fighting the temptation to use bad language by simply trying to stop. But she was never able to keep it up for long. She lived her Christian life feeling like a fraud, with a constant sense of guilt, a fear of praying aloud, and ashamed of her sinful past. She was plagued by doubts and insecurities. But as she listened to that talk, something clicked.

She had always known the truth that Christ had saved her from her sin, but she hadn't really grasped that he had done all that was necessary to make her totally righteous. She doesn't have to earn it or make up for her past failures. When she came to understand this truth recently, she was transformed! That truth set her free, changing not just her heart but her mouth—which is currently overflowing with excitement about Jesus!

I'm guessing that you've got some areas of your life that you're "working on". Perhaps it's a tendency towards some kind of sin that refuses to go away or a habit that's proving hard to break out of. In this chapter we're going to look at how biblical meditation can help us to fight sin and pursue obedience as we allow God's truth to work in our hearts.

EAT, SLEEP, SIN, REPEAT

My son used to have a cute t-shirt which read "Eat, sleep, surf, repeat". Our Christian life can feel like a similar cycle, only way more hopeless: eat, sleep, sin, repeat.

The slippery slide of sin is described in vivid detail in Psalm 1 v 1 as "[walking] in step with the wicked", "[standing] in the way that sinners take" and "[sitting] in the company of mockers". For the most part these images are not literal but metaphorical—they describe a disposition of the heart.

We get a literal(!) example of what this looks like in practice with Peter in Luke 22. As Jesus was being tried in the high priest's house, Peter really did sit down warming himself at the fire in the courtyard of those who had arrested his Lord. When challenged about his allegiance to Jesus, he said "I don't know him" (v 57)—*three times*. Once we're sitting comfortably with sinners, it is almost impossible to run from temptation. But sin always ends in tears. When Peter realised what he'd done, "he went outside and wept bitterly" (22 v 62).

I use the phrase "slippery slide", because at the top of the slide we are not doing anything wrong—to use the language of Proverbs 7, we're just walking down the street towards the wayward woman's house. Then we find ourselves standing at the door. Then we are sitting with her. Nothing wrong in that. Except that it's then impossible to run when temptation comes. We have deliberately set foot on a path that only has one ending: defeat. We can all resonate with Peter's breaking down and weeping bitterly—so how is it that the very next evening we are on that path again? Just walking near her house; just standing at her door; just sitting with her. "But this time it will be different because I have resolved not to do it again," we say to ourselves.

But you know how it always ends.

Resolve, walk, stand, sit, defeat, guilt, repeat.

Pause for a moment and think: Where do you see this repeated cycle of sin in your life?

BREAKING THE CYCLE

Meditating on the truth will break that cycle with a new word that we find in Psalm 1 v 2: delight.

> *Blessed is the one*
>   *who does not walk in step with the wicked*
> *or stand in the way that sinners take*
>   *or sit in the company of mockers,*
> *but whose delight is in the law of the LORD,*
>   *and who meditates on his law day and night.*
> *That person is like a tree planted by streams of water,*
>   *which yields its fruit in season*

and whose leaf does not wither—
whatever they do prospers. (Psalm 1 v 1-3)

As the very next psalm reminds us, as we take refuge in the Son, the wrath we deserve is taken by him on the cross (Psalm 2 v 12). We become those who are "blessed"—no longer following the way of sinners, but following the way of the righteous.

So meditation is putting our roots down deep into this reality: We do not sit, stand, walk in the way of sinners anymore. Yes, their company may feel familiar. But meditation is about remembering that we are changed. Jesus hasn't merely tamed us—he has transformed us and given us new hearts that love to walk in step with his Spirit. We are no longer those who love to watch pornography, or gossip in the office, or imagine ourselves in the arms of that friend at the school gate, or binge on chocolate every evening, or spend drinking fuelled nights out with mates, unable to serve God with a clear conscience the day after. That's not who we are anymore, so we no longer have to do those things. We are following the way of the righteous. We are blessed.

As we put our roots down deep into this truth through meditating on it, our desires are changed. I won't want to engage in that sin anymore when I realise how much it cost Jesus to die for what I keep on doing. When I understand that he has given me his perfect righteousness and set me on the way of righteousness with other brothers and sisters to help me, I find courage and strength to walk a different way; to swim upstream; to choose to do the right thing.

That's when the real fruit of obedience begins to grow in my life (v 3).

GETTING TO THE ROOT

Let's use some examples to explore how this works. Imagine I am struggling with feeling jealous of my friend. I could try fighting that by sticking the "fake fruit" of obedience on the outside of my life—smiling through gritted teeth and saying nice things to her face, while cursing her in my heart. And while that's better than cursing her to her face, it doesn't solve the real problem: my heart.

Meditation doesn't settle for fake fruit, but digs underneath to see what is at the root: what is the thinking that lies behind the feelings of jealousy?

What am I believing about God in this situation? Do I blame him, resent him, feel that he is withholding blessing from me, or unfairly blessing my friend and not me?

What am I believing about myself? That I have a right to what my friend has? That I deserve it for all that I have done for God? Or perhaps I despair and feel I will never be as good/attractive/tall/successful/wealthy/able to attract a partner as her? Or that life should be different, and I should have what she has?

What am I believing about my friend? That she doesn't deserve what she has, or doesn't appreciate it? That she is so sinful in other areas, I don't understand why she is blessed like this? Or that she is intrinsically better/more worthy/a stronger Christian than I am, and she makes me feel inferior and unworthy?

As we dig back to the roots of the sin, we begin to see the untruth that we have been believing.

This is where regularly using the meditation tool from section 2—especially chapter 6, Turn—can really help to train us in heart surgery. I have found that as I daily dig into my heart to see what lies I am believing, I have gotten to know my own heart better. So now when I have an extreme reaction to something—a sudden flash of jealousy or anger, say—I am better able to dig around and work out what wrong beliefs lie at the heart of that reaction.

THE FRUIT OF THAT ROOT

Having diagnosed the lies that we believe, we need to look at the consequences of believing those lies. We are easily duped into thinking that sin ends in delight, but Psalm 1 reminds us where sin really ends—in destruction:

> *Not so the wicked!*
> *They are like chaff*
> *that the wind blows away.*
> *Therefore the wicked will not stand in the judgment,*
> *nor sinners in the assembly of the righteous.*
> *For the LORD watches over the way of the righteous,*
> *but the way of the wicked leads to destruction.*
> *(Psalm 1 v 4-6)*

In the heat of the moment we think to ourselves, "I can ask for forgiveness later"—forgetting that sin always leads to destruction. And the choice that the gospel offers to us is that it is either our destruction, or Jesus'. He is "the one" that the first half of Psalm 1 describes in all his splendour: like a tree planted by streams of water, he put his roots down deep into the truths of God's word as Satan tempted him. And yet he was "cut down" on our behalf. We fight sin by looking at its consequences—at the cross.

Jesus died for that slip, that decision, that little white lie, that foolish click on a YouTube link. He took the punishment for every lie we believe, and for every truth we refuse to believe. He did that so that we can be set free—no longer enslaved to lies in our minds, but set free to believe and meditate on the truth that helps us fight the battle with sin.

REPLANTING IN THE TRUTH

Next we need to replace the old soundtrack with God's new soundtrack of truth: the soundtrack that is all about him not me; the soundtrack that loves others and wants the best for them, rather than being oriented around me and what is best for me; the soundtrack that truly is music to my ears.

For example, if I realise that I am jealous because my friend has a partner and I would love one, that helps to show me where I am not allowing God to fulfil my deepest longings and needs. I could meditate on the fact that I have been welcomed into the most intimate, wonderful love relationship ever known—that of Christ the bridegroom and his church. He is always with me and one day will take me to be with him face to face. This is the relationship that all other marriages are a pale reflection of.

Meditation is taking that truth—that marriage is a pale reflection of the intimate relationship I can enjoy with

God—and spending more time with him, my perfect lover. I could perhaps learn Psalm 34 v 10: "those who seek the LORD lack no good thing". Then I'll need to keep speaking that truth to myself when I feel the old feelings of jealousy resurfacing and I'm tempted to walk, stand and sit on that path again.

GROWING FRUIT IN CHRIST BY FEEDING ON TRUTH
What we put our roots down into determines what fruit we bear in our lives.

> *Blessed is the one ... whose delight is in the law of the LORD,*
>   *and who meditates on his law day and night.*
> *That person is like a tree planted by streams of water,*
>   *which yields its fruit in season*
> *and whose leaf does not wither—*
>   *whatever they do prospers. (Psalm 1 v 1-3)*

If I am meditating on the untruth that God is deliberately withholding from me something I deserve, that will bear the fruit of jealousy in my life. Sin withers me into useless chaff (the bit of plant left after the wheat has been harvested).

But Psalm 1 is so liberating. As I put my roots down deep into the truth that Christ perfectly meditated day and night, but was cut down for me, I can delight in God. He is growing me into a tree that is eternally secure, rooted, flourishing, prospering, and blessing others with the fruit that is growing in my life. That security, that truth, sets me free to rejoice in all that my friend has, without being jealous.

GETTING TO THE ROOT

Here's another example. For years I have struggled with prayer. Every new year I would resolve to pray more. But another year passed, and the problem was still there, unchanged.

I was trying to find the secret to praying more, and more deeply—I tried lists, apps, books. But they were all fake fruit. It wasn't until I had to teach a seminar on prayer that I really dug deep into why I didn't pray.

What was I believing about God? I had such a small view of God. It was as I started to read some Christian biographies that my sister-in-law sent for the kids that I realised how weak a view of God I had compared to spiritual giants like George Müller and Hudson Taylor. Only, they weren't spiritual giants at all. They were ordinary men who believed that God was the giant who could achieve far more than all they could dream or imagine. And as they prayed, he built an incredible house.

What was I believing about myself? The ugly truth is that I didn't feel that I needed God. I'm a competent person and I like to fix things myself. I just didn't realise how weak I was—how pathetic and futile all my efforts were. If the Lord doesn't build the house then I am labouring in vain (Psalm 127 v 1).

THE FRUIT OF THAT ROOT

What were the consequences of believing those lies? Sin doesn't end in delight, but destruction. So much of the "ministry" I was doing was not bearing fruit and growing because I was building it in my own strength.

How different Jesus was! He spent nights in prayer to God—the perfect Son of God sought to build nothing on his own but only what his Father wanted. So who am I to arrogantly think I can manage without praying?!

The sin of my prayerlessness ends in destruction: Jesus died for my arrogance. I need to own that and confess my sin, if I am going to really change.

REPLANTING IN THE TRUTH

What was the truth I needed to meditate on, to put my roots down deep into? Essentially that God is big and I am small; he is the one who builds, not me. I am weak, he is strong. Anything I achieve is only through him at work. Meditating on the immensity of God, and my own weakness, transformed my heart so that I realised I needed to pray.

GROWING FRUIT IN CHRIST BY FEEDING ON TRUTH

What we put our roots into determines what fruit we bear. I was putting my roots into the mantras of the world that I should be a strong, powerful, independent woman. That grew the fruit of not depending on God through prayer. I had to repent and see that in Christ's perfect dependence on our Father, I too could believe and obey this truth: only God builds. I began to more regularly ask him to do that, while trusting that any labour I do prayerfully is not in vain.

So what fruit is growing in your life? Maybe you know that you've spent 20 years working on your mouth. Don't try to change by sticking fake fruit on the outside. Trace the fruit back to the roots. Get your roots planted deep into the truth of God's word through meditation and see the fruit of obedience grow in season.

(Obey) **MEDITATION TOOL: OBEY**
Look for patterns of disobedience. Dig into what you are believing about God/yourself in that moment. Run to Christ for forgiveness, and for the power to think truth and bear the fruit of obedience.

PUTTING IT INTO PRACTICE
Work through these questions to help you fill in the table on page 138.

Getting to the root

- *What happened?* You cannot attack a generality—so pinpoint a specific situation.
- *How did you feel?* Anxious? Guilty? Bored? Jealous? Something else?
- *What were you thinking at the time? Why did you think that?* If you find it hard to dig down to the wrong thinking, try drawing a stick man in that situation with a speech bubble, and write some negative thoughts in the bubble—don't think too hard, the first thing you think of is fine. Psychologists call this "projecting", because the thoughts you write down are ones you are projecting from your own mind. Often they will tip you off to what is going on in your heart.

- *What untruth are you believing about God? What untruth are you believing about yourself?* Again, generalising is no good: "God is good, therefore I should stop being jealous…" Rationalising is no good either: "I suppose I should stop being unreasonable and making demands of God so I won't be jealous…" Instead you need to get to the heart of why you feel so upset, in order to move forwards.

The fruit of that root

- *What are the consequences of believing this lie?* Think about the punishment that this deserves—Jesus died for that sin. Repent.

Replanting in the truth

- *What truth specifically contradicts the lie that you have believed?* Ask God (and maybe another Christian) to teach you the truth that refutes the lie directly. It may be a Bible story, or a verse. The truth needs to contradict the lie in order for it to convict you, lift the burden of unbelief, and bring delight. You may need to go back to the untruth and do a bit more work to see exactly what you are believing that is wrong.

Growing fruit in Christ by feeding on the truth

- *How can you make sure you keep feeding on this truth?* A powerful technique I discovered through psychotherapy is to write the Bible truth—ideally a verse— on something you can have on your person, such as an elastic band on your wrist or a stone in your pocket. Every time you notice yourself walking with this sin (Psalm 1 v 1), swap wrists/move pockets, ask for forgiveness, and power to change your thinking. See that Christ has already perfectly obeyed, so in him, you can believe and obey. Put your roots down into this delightful truth. Research shows that as you notice and actually do something physical to correct negative thoughts, you will have them less frequently. Then instead of walking, standing and sitting with sinners, you will be actively delighting in God's word and growing its fruit in your life.

SINFUL EVENT	WHY?	UNTRUTH ABOUT GOD/MYSELF	CONSEQUENCES: REPENT!	TRUTH: ASK GOD TO TEACH YOU
I don't pray	I don't feel I need to	I don't need God	Jesus died for my arrogance	Unless the Lord builds the house, the labourers labour in vain
Jealous of my friend	She has a partner	God is unfair, withholding good from me	Jesus died for my refusal to believe in his goodness	God is good and loving and all I need is in him

CHAPTER 10

Remembering to
Hold Fast

I grew up in what I like to call the "footprints era"—a golden age of Christian kitsch. Christian bookshops were full of cutesy bookmarks, notebooks and posters bearing the image of kittens with balls of wool, loosely linked to a Bible verse. The latter were often pinned up outside churches, on noticeboards, where they became faded by the sun and slightly warped by the rain.

One very popular poster featured a poem, *Footprints*. In it a man dreams that he is walking along a beach as scenes from his life flash across the sky. As he looks back, he sees the footprints of him and God in the sand, but he is troubled by the fact that during the most difficult scenes of his life there is only one set of footprints. He asks God why he would leave him when he most needed him, and God replies: "My precious child … I would never leave you during your times of trial and suffering. When you saw only one set of footprints, it was then that I carried you." (Not, as my editor suggested, "It was then that I decided we should both hop"!)

There's a reason why that poem was so popular: almost all of us will go through seasons when life is hard and God feels far away.

Maybe it's when we're grieving the loss of a loved one or the lack of a relationship; when we're battling physical pain or emotional sorrow; when we're overwhelmed by doubt or depression or despair; when we're unmoored or unsettled by circumstances beyond our control. In these seasons, it's easy to begin to wonder where God is.

The Bible expresses a similar anguish in Psalm 77:

> *I cried out to God for help;*
> *I cried out to God to hear me.*
> *When I was in distress, I sought the Lord;*
> *at night I stretched out untiring hands,*
> *and I would not be comforted.*
> *I remembered you, God, and I groaned;*
> *I meditated, and my spirit grew faint.*
> *You kept my eyes from closing;*
> *I was too troubled to speak.*
> *I thought about the former days,*
> *the years of long ago;*
> *I remembered my songs in the night.*
> *My heart meditated and my spirit asked...*
> *(Psalm 77 v 1-6)*

The writer, Asaph, is so distressed that he cannot sleep or eat. His soul is on the edge of giving up. And what does he do? He meditates. As the psalm continues, meditation helps him to hold fast to God so that by the end of it, Asaph is able to confidently declare that God is a mighty rescuer, even "though [his] footprints were not seen" (v 19).

So how can we hold fast to God in times of trouble when his footprints are not seen? Psalm 77 doesn't give us a cute poster or whimsical poem but rather a raw account of the honest, painful questions that suffering brings. But into that rawness, meditation strikes a chord of hope…

HONEST QUESTIONS

How do you instinctively react when suffering comes?

Some of us become the victims of our own obsessive spiral of negative thoughts. We chew over them, meditating on them, powerless to break out. In the words of a character in John Green's novel, *Turtles All the Way Down*: "The thing about a [thought] spiral is, if you follow it inward, it never actually ends. It just keeps tightening, infinitely."

At the other extreme, some of us live in denial, maybe by distracting ourselves or keeping so busy that we don't have to think at all. Or perhaps we adopt the "mindful" approach and seek to live in the present, untouched by anything else, focusing only on the here and now and allowing negative thoughts to pass us by without being affected by them.

Biblical meditation could not be more different. Rather than being hopeless victims swept along by the pain or burying our heads in the sands of busyness, meditation enables us to engage with the grief and ask the difficult questions about why this has happened.

> *My heart meditated and my spirit asked:*
> *"Will the Lord reject for ever?*

> *Will he never show his favour again?*
> *Has his unfailing love vanished for ever?*
>   *Has his promise failed for all time?*
> *Has God forgotten to be merciful?*
>   *Has he in anger withheld his compassion?"*
> (Psalm 77 v 6-9)

Will he, will he, has he, has he, has he, has he?

Just as we have to be honest about a medical problem in order to get the right medication, Asaph is honest about the questions he really has: *Is God really loving? Has his promise failed? Has he forgotten?*

Often it helps to do this digging with someone else. I met with a close friend the other day. Her mum was recently diagnosed with cancer, her two sisters are both struggling with mental health, and she is dealing with her own life-threatening allergy crises. As we talked, I asked my friend, "What are the thoughts you are afraid to say out loud?" Her eyes welled up and tears spilled down her cheeks. She stammered, fumbled, and then finally admitted: "I just feel so angry at God. I've been through so much, he's taken so much from me, how can he take my mum as well?"

And that, right there, is where truth starts to heal. Saying out loud what is troubling us is often the first part of the cure.

So if you're going through the mill at the moment, be honest. What are your fears about God? What are your doubts about him? What are your grievances against him? Speak them out loud to him in prayer, and possibly to a mature Christian friend as well.

But don't stop there. The psalmist doesn't.

REMEMBER THE LORD

In verse 10 there is a massive shift in the mood of the psalm:

Then I thought, "To this I will appeal:
the years when the Most High stretched out his
right hand.
I will remember the deeds of the LORD;
yes, I will remember your miracles of long ago.
I will consider all your works
and meditate on all your mighty deeds."
(Psalm 77 v 10-12)

Being honest about his feelings is like opening a window in a stuffy room. All of a sudden Asaph seems to breathe in fresh air. As he digs into the root of the problem, he begins to see the truth he needs to remember about God.

There is a decisive change—the repeated phrase is no longer "Has he?" but "I will". We see a clear resolve: "I will remember the deeds of the LORD; yes, I will remember your miracles of long ago, I will consider all your works and meditate on all your mighty deeds" (v 11-12).

As I lie awake too troubled to sleep, I will not find my mind naturally drifting to all of God's deeds in the past. Meditation doesn't happen by chance; it happens by choice: "I will … yes, I will". Instead of thinking about all the ways I cannot see God right now, I must choose to remember Christ.

Our problem is not just that we don't remember. It's that we don't choose to remember. We don't realise that remembering is an act of the will: "Yes, I will remember". In the words of the 20th-century preacher Martin Lloyd Jones:

"Have you realised that most of your unhappiness in life is due to the fact that you are listening to yourself instead of talking to yourself?" Instead of continuing to be a victim of negative thoughts, we must instead remember what God has done, and what he is doing. We must talk truth back to ourselves. This is meditation, as we defined it right at the start: *talking with yourself in your heart.*

And here (again) is why a regular habit of meditation as seen in section 2 is so important: the truths we speak to ourselves will be the truths we have stored up from God's word. Then when the struggles come, we can open up the right Kilner jar and feed on the tomatoes we stored up for this particular battle.

Darlene Diebler Rose was a missionary who ended up on death row in a Japanese prisoner-of-war camp during World War Two. Forced to survive on just one meal a day of watery porridge with pebbles in it, she writes that it was remembering God's living word that sustained her:

> Starting with A, I would repeat a verse that began with that letter. I discovered that most of the songs we had sung when I was a little girl were still hidden in my heart, though I hadn't consciously memorised many of them … In the cell I was grateful now for those days in Vacation Bible School when I had memorised many single verses, complete chapters and psalms as well as whole books of the Bible …
>
> The Lord fed me with the Living Bread that had been stored against the day when fresh supply was

cut off by the loss of my Bible. He brought daily comfort and encouragement—yes, and joy—to my heart through knowledge of the word … I had never needed the Scriptures more than in those months on death row, but since so much of his word was there in my heart, it was not the punishment the Kempeitai [military police] had anticipated when they took my Bible. (*Evidence Not Seen*, p 129-130)

Here's another example from a little closer to home. Dorothy Spencer was a frail old lady I used to visit. As she was dying, during one visit, she said, "All those sermons, all those years, this is what they were for. Now is when I need those truths."

If you're reading this chapter in the "summer", start storing up those truths—learning them, recapping them, carefully bottling them up in Kilner jars, so that in the dark winter you have what you need to keep holding fast to God.

If you're reading this in the "winter"—wow, well done for managing to make sense of the words on this page! What are you struggling with right now? Dig deeper… ask your soul why it is downcast. Maybe try writing down why you feel like you do, or use the stick man technique from chapter 9—draw a sad stick man and a speech bubble and annotate his thoughts. Then speak to yourself: feed on Christ, remembering all that he has done.

A WORD TO THOSE IN WINTER

If all that seems too hard or too overwhelming right now, here are two truths to encourage you.

First, sometimes meditation just sounds like groaning. That's what Asaph says he's doing in verse 3. Groaning is the Bible's phrase to help convey what words cannot. When we're too troubled to speak—unable to find enough words to convey the pain of being, worn down by the inescapable sleepless, unending, relentlessness of it all—we can groan. As our spirit grows faint, the Spirit "testifies with our spirit" (Romans 8 v 16)—he comes alongside us and cries out on our behalf with groans that words cannot express (Romans 8 v 26).

Its ok to have no words, to be too weak. Meditation is remembering God in the pain, turning to him in our weakness, and allowing his Spirit to take us by the hand and together turn to God with wordless groans.

Remember my Danish friend's sister from chapter 2? Secular meditation was too hard for her; she was too sick. In the depths of despair there is no self-help technique that can lift you out of the pit. You need someone to climb down into the pit with you—someone who knows the deepest darkness of suffering. Meditation is remembering that the Lord has done precisely that.

Second, songs give us words when we have none. Growing up, I remember vividly my dad's favourite song, "Sad songs" by Elton John. The lyrics speak of sad songs reaching into your room, and how sometimes there are lines where every single word rings true, and it feels so good to have someone else express how it hurts.

In the darkness of the night, in the depths of winter, our minds are confused, bewildered, and overwhelmed. Sometimes you cannot even comprehend words on a page—it's like you can read the individual words and know they form a sentence, but you just can't understand what that sentence is saying. That makes it hard to read the Bible. So songs in the night are God's gift to those who lie unsleeping and uncomforted in the darkness.

That's why God has given us an entire songbook at the heart of the Bible. The psalms are songs which express every range of emotion. They give us not just words, but beautiful, God-given poetic words—words that don't just express truth but reach into your soul and cause it to sigh: "At last, someone who understands".

Ephesians and Colossians tell us that our singing doesn't need to be limited to the psalms in the Bible—"hymns" and "songs from the Spirit" can be sung too. I don't have space to tell you of the many Christian songs through which God has whispered his truth to me in the night. But I expect you may well have experienced this already—you just didn't know that it was called meditating!

REMEMBER THE DEEDS OF THE LORD

So biblical meditation during times of suffering digs to the root of our fears and resolves to remember the Lord. But what is it that we're to remember?

Psalm 77 v 11-12 tells us that Asaph looks back and remembers "the deeds of the LORD", his "miracles of long ago", "all [his] works" and "all [his] mighty deeds". He goes on to specifically recount God's redemption of his people from slavery in Egypt through the exodus and parting of the Red Sea (v 15-19). How much more do we have to remember?!

LINDA ALLCOCK

Hopefully you've guessed what's coming next. We can look back to the greatest act of redemption in all of history, when God sent his Son to die on a cross to save us from the waters of God's judgment and bring us safely into his kingdom. We can and we must remember Christ.

My friend's complaint was: "I just feel so angry at God. I've been through so much, he's taken so much from me—how can he take my mum as well?" In focusing on all that God has taken, it's easy to lose sight of all that he has given. But we'll find that this second list is actually endless as we begin to remember all that he has done, not just in our lifetime but throughout history. To put her doubts in perspective, this friend could meditate on the fact that God did not hesitate to give her the best thing he has—his one and only Son. Jesus faced death so that he could offer her, and her mother, forgiveness, and welcome her into a world without cancer or allergies or depression. Death will not be the last word.

The problem with despair, distress, doubt is that it can make us quite introspective. That is completely understandable. But as Asaph remembers God's deeds, works and miracles, his gaze is lifted from himself to God.

Your ways, God, are holy.
   What god is as great as our God?
You are the God who performs miracles;
   you display your power among the peoples.
(Psalm 77 v 13-14)

Secular meditation says that the treasure is within. But Asaph is very clear: God is the treasure, and his rightful place is at the centre of everything—of the universe, of these circumstances, of my thoughts. Thinking this way—thinking rightly—is what will free us from the trap of introspection.

REMEMBER CREATIVELY

But Asaph is not done yet. He continues to remember God's rescue through the exodus…

> *With your mighty arm you redeemed your people,*
> *the descendants of Jacob and Joseph.*
> *The waters saw you, God,*
> *the waters saw you and writhed;*
> *the very depths were convulsed.*
> *The clouds poured down water,*
> *the heavens resounded with thunder;*
> *your arrows flashed back and forth.*
> *Your thunder was heard in the whirlwind,*
> *your lightning lit up the world;*
> *the earth trembled and quaked.*
> *Your path led through the sea,*
> *your way through the mighty waters,*
> *though your footprints were not seen.*
> *(Psalm 77 v 15-19)*

God has given us an imagination for a reason. The psalmist uses his to create a beautifully poetic celebration of God's redemptive act. He imagines what it would have been like to be there as the waves writhed and convulsed, the earth trembled and quaked and God fought on behalf of his people to set them free.

There are examples in Scripture of people worshipping God through dance, poetry, needlework, and painting. Don't reduce meditation to chanting by rote—it can be a creative, imaginative remembering of what God has done. Plus there's something really powerful about getting lost in the creative process that helps our minds to recuperate in bleak situations—as we get into the flow we forget everything else. When I was recovering from depression, I would write songs to express God's truth. Most of them have never made it out of my journal, but that's not the point!

So what about you? How could you worship God creatively for the way he has rescued you? It might be writing a poem or drawing a picture or even choreographing a dance. Allow yourself to creatively worship God for the historical fact that he has set you free.

REMEMBERING LEADS US INTO COMMUNITY

There's one more verse in Psalm 77, and it's a bit of a strange one: "You led your people like a flock by the hand of Moses and Aaron" (v 20). I'm intrigued that Asaph ends his song that way. Surely it would have been much more dynamic to end at verse 19 with "though your footprints were not seen".

So why the "P.S."? I think his point is that in the suffering, though we do not see God's footprints, he is ministering to us through what we *can* see and hear—through human hands, and mouths. Whether we're suffering or celebrating, we can hear God's words from the lips of faithful friends.

And we can speak God's words to them in return. From Deuteronomy through to the New Testament, meditation in the Bible is never just about me—it's intended to strengthen our community: "Let the message of Christ dwell among you richly as you teach and admonish one another with all wisdom through psalms, hymns and songs from the spirit, singing to God with gratitude in your hearts" (Colossians 3 v 16). Much that we've considered about biblical meditation is personal and private, but as the message of Christ dwells in us richly, it cannot be contained—it will overflow to others. And often we'll find that it is God's kindness to us in hard times that we speak of most passionately.

MORE THAN FOOTPRINTS IN THE SAND

Psalm 77 offers us a better model for dealing with our sorrows than the footprints poem ever could. It's not twee; it's raw. What began with cries of despair ends with a confident declaration of God's saving power—even "though [his] footprints were not seen" (v 19).

Today, when we are looking for the footprints of God, we can look back in history to see them. God himself stepped into his world to lead his flock in the person of his Son, our Lord Jesus. If we had lived in the right place at the right time we could have seen him, touched him, smelled him, heard him—and yes, seen his footprints. He is real.

Meditation is more than just remembering truth. It is seeing Jesus. This is the hope we hold onto in trouble and hold out to those who are suffering—not a cute Bible-verse poster, but a man. The One who cried out in heart-rending gut-wrenching *honesty* on the cross: "My God, why have you forsaken me?" The One who *remembered* the Scriptures in the midst of suffering and submitted himself to slander so that they would be fulfilled. The One who knows what it is to *groan* in agony in the garden of Gethsemane. The One who *borrowed the words of songs* like Psalm 22 as he fulfilled everything that song spoke of. The One who endured the longest, darkest of times so that we would never have to.

Asaph considered all God's works (v 12)—but we have so much more we can consider! And as we consider him who endured the cross, we will not lose heart (Hebrews 12 v 3).

Hold fast
MEDITATION TOOL: HOLD FAST

In suffering, be honest with God. Remember that the Spirit groans with you. Choose to remember Christ. Remember through story and song. Let others in, to pray, listen and cry with you.

Conclusion

Psalm 119 has provided so much material for this book that it seems fitting to end in the same way that it does.

So after more than 170 verses extolling the virtues of God's word, how would you expect such a psalm to end? In ecstatic cries of delight, as the psalmist rides the giddy heights of his enlightened relationship with God?

Not quite…

> *I long for your salvation, LORD,*
> *and your law gives me delight.*
> *Let me live that I may praise you,*
> *and may your laws sustain me.*
> *I have strayed like a lost sheep.*
> *Seek your servant,*
> *for I have not forgotten your commands.*
> *(Psalm 119 v 174-176)*

These verses leave us with three final thoughts about meditation. *First, meditation is longing—not arriving* (v 174). The goal of Buddhist meditation is to arrive at the blissful, spiritual state of "nirvana". Yet in spite of continual delight in meditation, the psalmist has not arrived—he still longs for the Lord's salvation. He doesn't know it, but he is longing for Christ!

We have Christ, and yet in many respects we are still longing to possess by sight that which we currently enjoy by faith. Meditation makes us long more deeply to be with the One we think so much about. Richard Baxter describes this beautifully:

> When we come to die ... what a joy will it be to think, "I am going to the place from whence I tasted such frequent delights; to that God whom I have met in my meditation so often! [If] my spirits [were] so refreshed when I had but a taste, what will it be when I shall feed on it freely?"
> (*The Saints' Everlasting Rest*, p 191)

Second, meditation overflows into a life that praises God (v 175). Secular meditation promises inner calm, well-being and happiness—but it can easily become introspective. Biblical meditation could not be more different—as the Lord takes his rightful place at the centre of our thinking, we begin to orient our life around him. As we delight to think more and more about God, our delight cannot be contained—it overflows to others.

Third, meditation seeks the God who first sought us (v 176). Even after 175 verses of praise and prayer, the Psalmist admits: "I have strayed like a lost sheep".

"Then what hope is there for me?!" we might ask. "In comparison to the psalmist my devotional life is a complete shipwreck!"

There is every hope for you. Because your relationship with God does not rest on you seeking God—it rests on the fact that Christ came to seek and to save the lost (Luke 19 v 10). And as we make feeble attempts to meditate, we will stray. We will behave like foolish sheep. But God leads his flock. He is the One who sought us. He is the One who saves us. And we can know him deeper still. Meditation is seeking the God who first loved us.

Books Referenced

Richard Baxter, *The Saints' Everlasting Rest* (Kindle Edition, 2010)

Edmund Calamy, *The Art of Divine Meditation* (Tho. Parkhurst, 1680)

Darlene Diebler Rose, *Evidence Not Seen* (Harper Collins, 1998)

Derek Kidner, *Psalms 73 – 150,* Tyndale Old Testament Commentaries (IVP, 1975)

Thich Nhat Hanh, *The Miracle of Mindfulness* (Beacon Press, 1987)

John Owen, *The Grace and Duty of Being Spiritually Minded* (Kindle Edition, 2012)

Eckhart Tolle, *The Power of Now: A Guide to Spiritual Enlightenment* (New World Library, 2004)

Donald Whitney, *Spiritual Disciplines for the Christian Life* (Navpress, 1991)

Endnotes

[1] https://www.psychologytoday.com/gb/blog/your-brain-work/200910/easily-distracted-why-its-hard-focus-and-what-do-about-it, accessed 18 June 2019

[2] https://en.oxforddictionaries.com/definition/meditate, accessed 01 March 2019

[3] https://www.desiringgod.org/messages/meditate-on-the-word-of-the-lord-day-and-night, accessed 21 February 2020

[4] Paraphrased from *The Spiritual Exercises of St. Ignatius of Loyola*, available at https://archive.org/details/TheSpiritualExercisesIgnatius/page/n4/mode/2up, accessed 21 February 2020

[5] https://www.digitalinformationworld.com/2019/01/how-much-time-do-people-spend-social-media-infographic.html, accessed 25 June 2019

[6] www.ucl.ac.uk/museums-static/digitalegypt/amarna/belief.html, accessed 21 February 2020

Acknowledgements

Firstly, I must thank God for enabling me to learn how to meditate in the darkness of depression, and for kindly giving me ten years to recover before giving me the opportunity to write about it.

Huge thanks are due to my editor Rachel Jones, gifted not just in writing but also with patience, wisdom and humour. Some I will never be able to thank in this life but have learned much from are John Owen, Richard Baxter and Edmund Calamy—pastors and writers from the 17th century. Thanks to Clare Heath-Whyte, author and historian, for teaching me how to find, access, search and read historical documents online. I'm indebted to lecturers David Green and Garry Williams at London Seminary for allowing me to pick their brains over lunch about various parts of the meditation tool. Also to Julian Hardyman, Carl Laferton and Johnny Prime for looking over this manuscript and challenging and encouraging me.

Lastly, my thanks go to my kids for helping me to learn to meditate in spite of noise, chaos and mess! (If I can do it, you can too.) Underpinning all of this has been my best friend, mentor and example—Jonty—encouraging me to make things clearer, simpler and always centred on Christ.

thegoodbook
COMPANY

BIBLICAL | RELEVANT | ACCESSIBLE

At The Good Book Company, we are dedicated to helping Christians and local churches grow. We believe that God's growth process always starts with hearing clearly what he has said to us through his timeless word—the Bible.

Ever since we opened our doors in 1991, we have been striving to produce Bible-based resources that bring glory to God. We have grown to become an international provider of user-friendly resources to the Christian community, with believers of all backgrounds and denominations using our books, Bible studies, devotionals, evangelistic resources, and DVD-based courses.

We want to equip ordinary Christians to live for Christ day by day, and churches to grow in their knowledge of God, their love for one another, and the effectiveness of their outreach.

Call us for a discussion of your needs or visit one of our local websites for more information on the resources and services we provide.

Your friends at The Good Book Company

thegoodbook.com | thegoodbook.co.uk
thegoodbook.com.au | thegoodbook.co.nz
thegoodbook.co.in